# HANDEL *Lamps*

## Painted Shades & Glassware

A Limited Edition

Robert De Falco

Carole Goldman Hibel

John Hibel

H&D press

Library of Congress Catalog Card Number 84-62544
ISBN Number 0-9614223-0-0

Copyright 1986 by H & D Press, Inc.
Published by H & D Press, Inc.
Staten Island, New York
All Rights Reserved
Printed in The United States of America

*For Our Parents . . .*
*Anthony C. DeFalco*
*Helen Bossack*
*Michael Bossack*
*David Goldman*
*Shirley Goldman*
*Dora Hibel*

# ACKNOWLEDGEMENTS

We wish to express our gratitude to several people who have made special contributions to this book:

Chris Revi, who inspired us and offered his friendship, knowledge, and support every step of the way . . .

Dominic D'Agostino, of Qualigraphics, whose patient guidance, skill and faith in this project were invaluable . . .

Michael Ottavi, whose mutual enthusiasm and friendship have supported us over the years . . .

Ruth S. Goldman, who provided editorial assistance, and helped sustain us with her interest and encouragement . . .

David and Agnes Baur, who were kind enough to share with us information and original documentation, as well as their personal feelings and recollections . . .

Stuart Keith (Department of Ornithology, American Museum of Natural History, New York City), who identified the 'painted birds' . . .

Thomas H. Everett (Senior Horticulture Specialist, The New York Botanical Garden, Bronx, New York) and Rupert Barneby (Curator, The New York Botanical Garden, Bronx, New York), who identified the 'painted flowers and trees' . . .

Special thanks are also due the following people, who assisted and supported us in this endeavor:

John Kisch-Photography, Nicholas I. Dawes, Karen L. Wellikoff, Jerome Goldman, Frank Wisniewski, Henry 'Hank' Hoff, Rusty Nielsen, Mr. & Mrs. A. Trachtenberg, Mr. & Mrs. R. Campagnola, Deborah Sallero

# BIBLIOGRAPHY

Curtis, George Munson, *A Century of Meriden*. Journal Publishing Co., 1906.

Revi, Albert Christian, *American Art Nouveau Glass*. Thomas Nelson Inc., 1968.

Revi, Albert Christian, *Nineteenth Century Glass*. Thomas Nelson Inc., 1959.

*" . . . Everything dies baby that's a fact*
*But maybe everything that dies*
*Someday comes back . . . "*
                                    Bruce Springsteen

# INTRODUCTION

From its inception in 1885 to its closing in 1936, The Handel Company of Meriden, Connecticut produced quality decorative items for the home. For the most part they were successful in this effort, especially with their charming, and sometimes flamboyant, lamps with hand painted glass shades. It is for these lamps that they will be best remembered by collectors and art historians.

In his youth, Philip Julius Handel manifested a strong business acumen which served him well in later years. He was able to draw to himself a group of local artists who all demonstrated a higher degree of talent than would be expected from a sleepy Connecticut community that based its economy on the manufacture of various kinds of household goods. This small group of artists banded together, forming a loose-knit society with their own publication, *Under The Shade*, and Handel's designers, too, published their own magazine which they called *Artgum-ption*. Obviously, both departments had acquired a sense of 'family', which was encouraged by the owners of the Company.

During and after The Handel Company's existence, many of these artists left to enter into businesses of their own, some of them leaving their own imprint on the community's art history. Many of the Handel decorated glass shades bear their signatures, e.g., Henry Bedigie, Albert Parlow, William Runge and George Palme, to name but a few. Lamps with shades bearing these signatures will always command a premium price on the art glass market. The designs painted on these shades run the gamut from delicate florals to exotic birds and scenes of faraway places, but it is only when they are lit that their true beauty is revealed.

Like many other early 20th century creations, the beauty of Handel's products were forgotten for years, with only a few people still retaining them as part of their lives and homes. They came into their own again after Tiffany's leaded glass lamps got beyond the reach of collectors of modest means. Now Handel lamps, too, are fetching unheard of prices on the art market. Even the less sophisticated designs, described in Handel catalogues and advertisements as 'library lamps', suitable for the stodgy, businesslike atmosphere of men's club's, are now becoming popular and are commanding strong prices.

Clearly, Handel's highly decorated lamps are fast gaining in popularity with sophisticated collectors. Those illustrated in this book present the reader with a full view of these handcrafted shades and bases, encompassing and defining the broad scope of artistic works that were produced in the Handel workshops. These very talented painters followed motifs supplied by their colleagues in the design department; however, no two shades are exactly alike and each shows individualistic nuances, depending upon the painter's expertise and talent.

John and Carole Hibel and Robert DeFalco are to be congratulated for assembling this monograph on Handel lamps and other decorated Handel objects. Over the many years that they have been collecting Handel products they have refined their taste, sharing their considerable knowledge with others in these pages. For both the novice and the experienced Handel collector, this volume will be an invaluable reference tool, as well as a book to enjoy for the sheer pleasure of viewing these unique works of art. The result of many years of research and study, this book will be acknowledged as the definitive work on the painted lamps and glassware of The Handel Company.

Albert Christian Revi
Hanover, Pennsylvania
November 1984

# TABLE OF CONTENTS

*CHAPTER I* . . . . . . . . . . . . . . . . . . . . . . . . . . . . . .  *7*
The Handel Company of Meriden, Connecticut

*CHAPTER II* . . . . . . . . . . . . . . . . . . . . . . . . . . . . .  *16*
Shade Types and Preparation Techniques
Handel Artists and Artisans
Bases and Metalwork

*CHAPTER III* . . . . . . . . . . . . . . . . . . . . . . . . . .  *42*
Handel Ware and Teroma Art Glass

*CHAPTER IV* . . . . . . . . . . . . . . . . . . . . . . . . . .  *44*
Handel Marks and Design Numbers

*LANDSCAPES* . . . . . . . . . . . . . . . . . . . . . . . . . .  *49*

*SEASCAPES* . . . . . . . . . . . . . . . . . . . . . . . . . . .  *99*

*BIRDS* . . . . . . . . . . . . . . . . . . . . . . . . . . . .  *121*

*FLOWERS* . . . . . . . . . . . . . . . . . . . . . . . . . . .  *149*

*BOUDOIRS* . . . . . . . . . . . . . . . . . . . . . . . . . . .  *179*

*DESK/PIANO LAMPS/MISCELLANY* . . . . . . . . . . . . . . .  *203*

*TEROMA ART GLASS* . . . . . . . . . . . . . . . . . . . . . .  *219*

*HANDEL WARE* . . . . . . . . . . . . . . . . . . . . . . . . .  *235*

# CHAPTER I

## THE HANDEL COMPANY OF MERIDEN, CONNECTICUT

Meriden was a thriving center of the lighting manufacturing industry in the late 19th century and an established center of decorative art production, notably metalware and lamps. In 1890 the town's largest employer was the Meriden Britannia Company, one of several silver and plate manufacturers who, in 1898, amalgamated to form the International Silver Company. Lamp makers and glass decorators included the Bradley and Hubbard Company, A.J. Hall and Company, and Edward Miller and Company. Much of Meriden's industry had been established in the wake of the Philadelphia Centennial Exhibition of 1876. This exhibition had a stimulating effect on the production of decorative art in America and spawned a variety of artistic workshops across the country, including Louis Comfort Tiffany's studios in New York (1879), and the Rookwood Pottery in Ohio (1880).

It was in this artistically turbulent and stimulating climate, in 1885, that the young Philip Handel (pronounced *Han'del*) formed a partnership with Adolph Eydam and established the "Eydam and Handel Company" in a building on the corner of Miller and Catlin streets in Meriden.

**Figure 1**   Philip J. Handel

Philip Handel was born in Meriden in 1867, a third generation member of the large German immigrant population who settled the central Connecticut farmland during the mid 19th century. His father, Jacob Handel, moved to Meriden from rural East Hartford in the early 1860's and worked as a foreman at the Charles Parker Company. Following his father's death in 1875, Philip helped to support his family by doing printing on a small scale. At the age of fourteen he left school and served a short apprenticeship at the Meriden Britannia Company, followed by five years of employment at the Meriden Flint Glass Company. It was during this period at the glassworks that Handel acquired the skills and knowledge of glass decorating techniques necessary to begin his own concern, and it was also there that he met Adolph Eydam, who was two years his senior and a talented member of Meriden's glassworking community.

Eydam and Handel began with a handful of employees recruited from Meriden's population of itinerant artists and decorators, most of whom lived in rooming houses for only one or two seasons. One of their earliest advertisements indicates that output was limited to a small range of useful and ornamental

**Figure 2**   Antone E. Teich

opal glassware, with lamp shades listed as the principal product (Figure 3). Blank glass was purchased from a number of sources, including the Gill Glass Company and the Roederfer Brothers Glassworks in Ohio and the Gleason Tiebout Works in New York City.

In the mid 1880's, oil or kerosene lamps were in widespread use domestically, together with gas lighting fixtures. Electric lamps were a costly rarity, Edison's incandescent bulb having only been perfected in 1879. Thus, the majority of Eydam and Handel's earliest shades were of the globular or hemispherical type, which were fitted on bases made by several local manufacturers.

In 1890 Philip Handel married Caroline Sutterlin, an employee who worked in the decorating shop. By this time the Company had begun to establish a reputation for good quality work and to specialize in painted lamp shades. Output increased as demand grew for new electric lamps and fixtures, and the Company made its first expansive move, opening a retail showroom at 18 College Place in New York City (Figure 4). Products included shades of all types and a new line of "reck decorated" (hand decorated) items, which reflected the public's taste for fine workmanship and the popular ideals of the Arts & Crafts movement.

**EYDAM & HANDEL CO.,**
**DECORATORS OF OPAL GLASSWARE,**
— SUCH AS —
**Lamp Shades, Vases, Jardinieres, Plaques, Salts, Etc.,**
OF FINEST QUALITY.
MANUFACTURERS FURNISHED WITH SPECIAL DESIGNS.
**Factory, Miller St., cor. Catlin, Meriden, Ct.**

Figure 3   Ad from *Meriden City Directory,* 1886

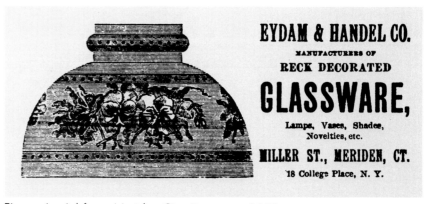

Figure 4   Ad from *Meriden City Directory,* 1890

The founding partnership broke up in 1892 when Adolph Eydam moved to the rival company of C.F. Monroe to assume the position of foreman. Shortly thereafter, Handel's workshops were moved from their original location to larger and more modern premises at 381 East Main Street, where the Company remained until it closed. Production continued for a six year period under the name "Philip J. Handel" (Figure 5) and the firm was known as "Handel and Company" from about 1898. On June 11, 1903 it became "The Handel Company Incorporated", with Philip J. Handel (Figure 1), Antone E. Teich (Figure 2), and Albert M. Parlow named as officers in the certificate of incorporation.

## PHILIP J. HANDEL,

(Successor to EYDAM & HANDEL Co.)

### Artistic Lamp Manufacturer,

**RICHLY DECORATED LAMP SHADES, SALTS, PEPPERS, AND OTHER NOVELTIES.**

Office and Salesroom, 381 East Main St., beyond Broad St.

### MERIDEN, CONN.

**Figure 5**    Ad from *Meriden City Directory*, 1892

Despite the premature death of his wife in 1904, Philip Handel continued in the role of chief administrator and principal designer, directing his energies toward the building of a successful company. He understood the dangers of limited output and heavy competition, and pursued a strategy of increased product lines coupled with greater in-house production and high quality art and design work. Incorporation and the subsequent injection of new operating capital led to the introduction of a wide variety of new products over the next decade. A range of leaded and simulated leaded glass shades, lamps and light fixtures were manufactured (including several designed by Philip Handel) and examples were exhibited at the St. Louis Exhibition of 1906.

The policy of in-house production led to the establishment of a foundry and casting shop by 1902, which was under the supervision of Antone Teich by the following year. The foundry was conceived by Philip Handel for the manufacture of his own lamp bases. The first castings were bases and lamp brackets, after designs patented in 1902 by Handel and his colleague, George Lockrow. The facility's rapid growth led to the manufacture of a wide variety of decorative metalware, including the mounts for light fixtures and opal glass items, bookends, door knockers, candlesticks and even handles for funeral caskets. The foundry's success was immediate and production rapidly surpassed the demands of the Company for its other products, which led to commercial metalware production. Handel's foundry supplied many other decorating workshops with lamp bases, and became an important branch of the Company's retail trade. The foundry gave The Handel Company an important economic advantage, promoting them from a "decorating workshop" status to a full-fledged manufactory. An advertisement from 1907 announced this important development to the public, stating that " . . . the equipment and facilities of The Handel Company are complete for the creation of the finished lamp from the crude materials."

The Company was enjoying a period of peak demand and rapid expansion in 1907, which continued until the beginning of the First World War. New lines were introduced and the premises was enlarged annually. Scores of patents were taken out, many of them by Philip Handel, including several lamp shade designs which were adapted from early kerosene models for use with electrical appliances.

Philip Handel died on July 14, 1914 at the age of forty eight. His second wife, Fanny Hirschfeld Handel, whom he had married in 1906, assumed her husband's role as president and treasurer of the Company and took an active part in the business during the lean years of World War I. She remarried in 1918, officially relinquishing management of the firm to Handel's cousin, William F. Handel, in 1919. William Handel had worked for the Company for a number of years and had been personally responsible for several commercially successful patent lamp designs. He was a sound business practicioner and gained the respect of the Handel work force.

The years immediately following World War I were the most prosperous in the history of The Handel Company. Fuelled by the genius of Ernest Lewis, head designer, and an impressive group of skilled and dedicated artists, craftsmen and administrators, the Company manufactured electric lamps of every description for the libraries, living rooms and boudoirs of an affluent, leisure-seeking post-war generation.

William Handel, who had been director of sales at The Handel Company before he became president, applied his marketing skills to the painted shade table lamps which had become the Company's trademark and leading seller. A sales campaign of unprecedented proportion was initiated, aimed at the affluent middle classes. A national network of sales representatives was established, consisting mostly of jewelry, lighting fixture, furniture and better department stores. They each carried a small selection of lamps and processed orders from an illustrated catalogue of the Company's current products. In order to maximize the retailers' impact they were supplied with particular models of lamps for display which were advertised simultaneously in leading periodicals, including *Harper's Bazaar, House and Garden, Good Housekeeping, House Beautiful, Vogue and Scribner's Magazine* (Figures 6-11). The advertising campaigns were concentrated during the fall and winter months when greater indoor activity and shorter daylight hours increased the demand for lighting.

The commercial success enjoyed by William Handel's administration was, however, short lived. The Company relied heavily on the buying power of middle income families, which was

SUMMER time, summer furniture, summer lamps! The cool pastel shades and restful tans are colors which lend themselves well to the making of Handel Lamps that serve on summer evenings. In the veranda picture, is table lamp number 6931, pendant lamp number 6894—both equally as useful and ornamental indoors. A variety of boudoir, desk, piano or floor lamps are conveniently numbered in the small panel—each the individual product of an artist—a craftsman.

Follow your desire to own a Handel Lamp. Its beauty will never fade. Go to the Handel dealer near you and make your selection. There is a Handel Lamp for every corner.

THE HANDEL COMPANY, Meriden, Conn.

# HANDEL *Lamps*

**Figure 6** Ad for design number 6931; *House Beautiful*, June 1922

RICHNESS of color, grace of form, and beauty of design are embodied in every Handel Lamp. And the delight which the possession of one brings, is a lasting one; for a Handel Lamp becomes a permanent part of your home—treasured as your oriental rugs and first editions.

The lamp shown is No. 6852. Look for Handel name on every lamp. Write for booklet of "Suggestions".

THE HANDEL COMPANY, Meriden, Conn.

**Figure 7** Ad for design number 6852;
*Century Magazine,* November 1920

HANDEL *Lamps*

The beauty, dignity, and rich coloring of Handel Lamps are the inspiration of artists who glory in creating. Their fashioning from durable materials is entrusted only to the skill of master craftsmen. And so a Handel Lamp is a lasting, delightful part of your home. The lamp illustrated is Number 6785.

Look for Handel name on every lamp. A dealer near you has them. His name on request.

THE HANDEL COMPANY, 380 EAST MAIN STREET, MERIDEN, CONN.

**Figure 8** Ad for design number 6785;
*Review of Reviews,* May 1920

# HANDEL *Lamps*

NOTHING adds so much to the cheerful attractiveness of a room as beautiful lamps. They add a decorative effect that is pleasingly distinctive. The lamplit room is one which best expresses the true charm of home.

Nowhere will you find such a wealth of original and lovely lamps as in the Handel Lamps. There are designs to harmonize with every type of furnishings; designs for living room, sun parlor and porch, for vestibule or bedroom. There is a grace of line, a harmony between shade and standard, an individuality in the colorful shade decorations

of Handel Lamps that is most unusual and artistic. Each is the work of master craftsmen, skilled in the art of creating beautiful things. All Handel Lamps are made for permanence. With ordinary care, they will last a lifetime.

The Table Lamp No. 7010 and pendant No. 7007 in the above illustration give a suggestion of the exquisite Handel designs. At the bottom are smaller lamps for dressing table, piano or for decorative use. These and many other lovely ones may be seen at better dealers everywhere. The Handel name is on every genuine Handel Lamp.

**THE HANDEL COMPANY**
Meriden, Conn.

**Figure 9** Ad for design number 7010; *House Beautiful*, June 1923

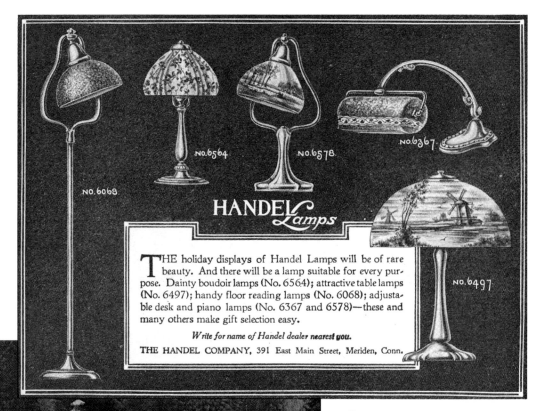

**Figure 10**
Ad from *Harper's Magazine*,
December 1917

**Figure 11**    Ad for design number 6778; *House Beautiful*, December 1919

rapidly diminished during the 1920's and virtually eliminated with the onset of the Great Depression. The Company's gradual decline was evidenced as early as 1922, when William Handel began a well-organized but costly regional sales campaign in an attempt to widen the market place for the Company's products and attract new distributors. Under the direction of John McGrath, sales manager, a team of travelling salesmen organized promotional displays in hotels throughout the Northeast, Mid-Atlantic, Southeast and Midwest regions of the country, showing dozens of lamps at each venue. Despite the efforts of William Handel and his dedicated staff, the economic situation caused the gradual reduction of the Company's work force, product lines and standards, and led to its eventual closing. The manufacture of painted shades and other luxury items had all but ceased by about 1929, although the Company continued to struggle through the early years of the 1930's with sales of inexpensive decorated china, earthenware products and lower priced lighting fixtures.

All production ceased in 1936, when William Handel announced the Company's closing. The corporation was finally and officially terminated in 1941.

# CHAPTER II

## SHADE TYPES AND PREPARATION TECHNIQUES

## HANDEL ARTISTS AND ARTISANS

## BASES AND METALWORK

## SHADE TYPES AND PREPARATION TECHNIQUES:

The Handel mark appeared on every type of glass and metal light fixture imaginable during the Company's production history, including globes of every description, panelled shades in colored slag glass, sometimes cleverly encased in decorative metal frames (the 'Teroca' technique), leaded shades and hand painted shades, which became the Company's most successful product. Handel's painted shades fall into two main categories: opal, or translucent glass examples of milky color, painted on the exterior only and chiefly used on library lamps or less expensive fixtures, and the interior, or reverse painted 'Teroma' shades, which were created from clear blown glass blanks, and are regarded by today's collectors as the most desirable product of The Handel Company.

No glass was ever made at The Handel Company's Meriden works. The earliest shades decorated by Handel were of standard type and supplied by glassworks in New York and the Midwest. The main source was the Roederfer Brothers glassworks in Bellaire, Ohio, which continued to supply The Handel Company throughout its history. During the years 1910-1914, many shades were purchased from German factories, however, examples stamped 'GERMANY' also appeared on lamps that were not produced until 1923. By the turn of the century The Handel Company began to design its own shades, with Philip Handel and George Lockrow acting as chief designers. The tradition of exclusive shade designs continued into William Handel's administration and he introduced a number of them himself, including an 18 inch domical shade molded with eight vertical lobes. The Handel Company's casting shop, where molds for lamp bases and other metalwork were made, supplied the glassworks with plaster of Paris master molds of the shades to be made.

Blank shades were brought to the factory packed in hay to prevent breakage. The majority were of simple form (domical or conical), though a few pattern-molded examples were designed and used to add variety to a line. The transformation of a blank into a decorative shade normally took one to two weeks and required the attention of up to a dozen individual craftsmen. The first stage for Teroma lamp shades was the creation of the patent 'chipped ice' effect, achieved by sand blasting and then coating the shade with fish glue and placing it in a kiln fired at 800°F. The contraction of the glue during the cooling stage tore away fragments of the glass surface, leaving a frosted, lightly textured effect when cleaned. Philip Handel took out a patent for the process in 1904, but the 'chipped' glass effect was not a new idea. Iced effects on glassware had been patented in England in 1883 by Carl Pieper for Dunkel and Compagnie of Germany, and by Eugene A. Savary of New Jersey in 1893. Chipping sometimes required more than one firing to achieve the right amount of surface texturing, and was occasionally highlighted by the addition of colored patination at a later firing. After the chipping kiln was unpacked, shades were placed in a steam bath to remove excess glue. Only blank shades were subjected to the chipping process, as this was the stage in production when the greatest number of 'wasters' occured and finished shades were too valuable to risk. The Handel Company exercised rigorous quality control throughout the entire preparation and decorating process, and most imperfect shades were discarded.

While the great majority of shades were 'chipped', some were also 'sand-finished', a surface treatment which added texture and depth to the shade. The process involved scattering tiny beads of colored glass onto the shade, which adhered permanently during firing. Sand-finishing was carried out during the final enamel-fixing firing. This relatively common practice should not be confused with the texturing effect used on the unique aquarium lamp (Page 117), which was achieved by coating the shade surface with globules of vitreous white enamel prior to the final firing.

# HANDEL ARTISTS AND ARTISANS:

After the shades had been prepared in the kilns they were sent to the decorating department, where their transformation was completed. During the early years of production George Lockrow supervised all art and design, but Albert M. Parlow assumed command of the decorating department at the new works when he joined the Company in 1903. Parlow served as Handel's chief designer and decorator until the late 1920's.

The printing department, where the transfer printing of Handel Ware and shades for lamps was carried out, was under the supervision of Julius Runge. Under his direction were Agnes Bauer (who was also a decorator) and her sister, Elizabeth Bauer (who was also a secretary). A third sister, Harriet Bauer, was a stenographer and, although she did draw some sketches and cartoons for the Company's magazine, *Under The Shade*, she never decorated a lamp. Other early printing department employees included Ms. Kelsey and Ms. Rebscher, who also worked as decorators.

In the early 1900's, Julius Runge left The Handel Company to work for the A.J. Hall Company and was not replaced until 1915, when Adolph Eydam returned to Handel to head this small group of workers. The size of the department kept increasing as the number of lamps designed for stencilling increased.

Opal glass blanks, decorated on the exterior only, were frequently of border pattern and required a minimum of artistic attention. In contrast, interior painted shades were decorated by a select group of highly skilled men and women, some of whom also acted as designers. Albert Parlow was among the most talented painters and his signature appears on a wide variety of lamp shades and other products during his long tenure with the Company. Henry Bedigie, a Frenchman, was another of Handel's finest and most prolific painters. Unlike many of his colleagues, Bedigie did not specialize in any particular subject, but applied his remarkable talent to a wide range of designs. Another of the better artists was Julius Runge's brother, William, considered by Ernest Lewis to be Handel's finest decorator. John Bailey, an Englishman, was another of Handel's gifted artists who created many of the large scenic shades, together with his fellow countryman, Arthur Cunette, a decorator in his own right who regularly 'filled in' (added background decoration) for Bailey. George Palme, a German glass craftsman, joined the work force in 1919 and, aside from the many reverse painted shades he decorated, introduced and was responsible for the decoration of overlay, or acid-etched, glass for shades and vases. Mr. F. Gubisch, originally from Holland, worked under

Palme and also specialized in this method of decoration. Peter Broggi was a Dutch artist who specialized in the decoration of shades with bird and floral motifs and, like many other of the Handel painters (Figures 12-21), was an accomplished artist.

**Figure 12**
**Gustave Reiman**
'Lowland Landscape with Windmill'
*Watercolor on paper*
*Signed lower right and dated 1904*
*4 in. × 13½ in. (10 cm. × 34.5 cm.)*

**Figure 13**
**Gustave Reiman**
'River Landscape with Punt'
*Watercolor on paper*
*Signed lower right and dated 1903*
*5¾ in. × 11¾ in. (14.5 cm. × 30 cm.)*

Figure 14

Figure 15

**Figure 14**
**Fred Matzow**
'Rocky Shore and Surf'
*Oil on canvas*
*Signed lower left and dated 1913*
*13½ in. × 27½ in. (34.5 cm. × 70 cm.)*

**Figure 15**
**Fred Matzow**
'Woodland Stream in Springtime'
*Oil on canvas*
*Signed lower left and dated 1913*
*23¼ in. × 11¼ in. (59 cm. × 28.5 cm.)*

**Figure 16**
**Edith M. Clark**
'Rocks at Money Island, Connecticut'
*Watercolor on paper*
*Inscribed on verso, dated 1903,*
*titled and located*
*Meriden, Connecticut*
*4¾ in. × 7 in. (12 cm. × 18 cm.)*

**Figure 17**
**Emil Melchior**
'Study of Apple Blossom'
*Watercolor on paper*
*Signed lower right and dated 1893*
*4¼ in. × 6¾ in. (11 cm. × 17 cm.)*

Figure 16

Figure 17

Figure 18

Figure 19

**Gustave Reiman**
'Autumn Landscape with Pond' and 'River Landscape'
A pair of pictures
*Watercolor on paper*
*Unsigned, Circa 1903*
*5½ in. × 17 in. (14 cm. × 43 cm.)*

**Figure 20**
**Peter Broggi**
'Country Lane'
*Oil on canvas*
*Signed lower left*
*24 in. × 20 in. (60 cm. × 50 cm.)*

**Figure 21**
**Albert M. Parlow**
'Golden Glow Evening'
*Watercolor on paper*
*Signed and titled on the mat, Circa 1915*
*5 in. × 8 in. (13 cm. × 20 cm.)*

*Albert Parlow was preeminent among the Handel artists during the first quarter of the century. This watercolor is typical of the bucolic landscapes he depicted on scenic shades.*

In addition to those previously mentioned, other members of the decorating and design departments include:

Edie Allard
Anderson
Baumgarter
Gussie Bouvie
Josephine Brazeau
Theodore Burghoff
Willa Caseth
Rowena Cheney
Grace Childs
Edith M. Clark (Owen)
Mollie Flanagan
Ray Freemantle
Elliott Gardner
R. Gillern
Robert Godwin
Arthur Hall
Heitland
Harry E. Homan
Hans Hueber
Elsie Jordan (Freemantle)

Barbara Lee
Florence Lewis
Gustave Loehner
Lilian Mackay
Fred Matzow
H. Mayer
Emil Melchior
Jules Meyers
George Mosher
Corinne Norbert
Mary Palme
Carl W. Puffee
Gustave Reiman
Rochette
Hattie Runge
Margaret Sinon
George Slater
Marie Walters
Katherine Casey Welch

A selection of artists' signatures are illustrated and identified, as follows (Figures 22-37):

**Figure 22**  Parlow

**Figure 26**  Rochette

**Figure 23**  Bailey

**Figure 27**  Bedigie

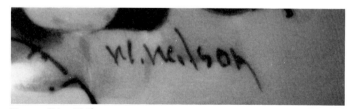

**Figure 24**  Wilson

**Figure 28**  Palme

**Figure 25**  Mosher

**Figure 29**  Gubisch

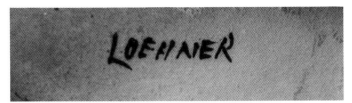

**Figure 30** Loehner

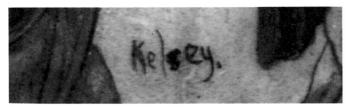

**Figure 31** Kelsey

**Figure 32** Broggi

**Figure 33** Runge

**Figure 34** Lewis

**Figure 35** Bauer

**Figure 36** Rebscher

**Figure 37** Godwin

The designs for painted shades originated from a separate art and design department, which was under the direction of Ernest C. Lewis during the Company's most productive period. The department's principal function was to supply the decorating department with working watercolor drawings of new designs, including specifications regarding dimensions, colors, techniques, kiln firing sequence, desired finish, etc. (Figures 38-43). Simpler patterns or pattern sections were designed for stencilled production, and an increasing number of shades were decorated in this manner during the 1920's, using paper templates and stencils made in the design department. This department was also responsible for producing all art work and layouts for The Handel Company's advertisements and brochures (Figures 44-48).

After preparation in the design department, a working sketch was sent to the decorating department to be copied by a painter onto a lamp shade. The artist followed the exact instructions specified on the sketch and the completed shade was then used as a sample by the other artists. A complex shade could take several days to pass through the decorating stage, sometimes requiring the attention of more than one artist, as well as several firings at various stages of production. The shades were placed upside down to allow the painters to decorate the interior. A spectrum of specially prepared colors was used, including the unique 'Crystal' paint which consisted of tiny colored glass particles mixed as a pigment.

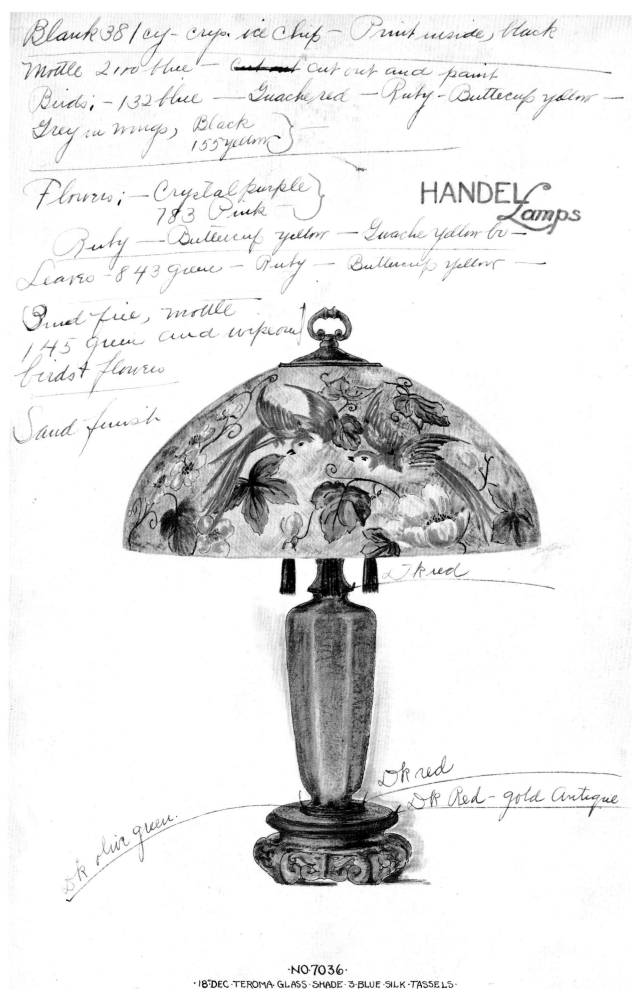

Blank 381 cy- crys. ice chip - Print inside, black
Mottle 2100 blue - ~~cut out~~ cut out and paint
Birds; - 132 blue - Guache red - Ruby - Buttercup yellow -
Grey in wings, Black
155 yellow }-

Flowers; - Crystal purple }
783 Pink }-
Ruby - Buttercup yellow - Guache yellow br -
Leaves - 843 green - Ruby - Buttercup yellow -

Qnd fire, mottle
145 green and wipeout }
birds & flowers

Sand finish

HANDEL Lamps

Dk red

Dk olive green.

Dk red
Dk Red - gold Antique

·NO·7036·
·18"·DEC·TEROMA·GLASS·SHADE·3·BLUE·SILK·TASSELS·
·BLUE·GROUND·BLUE&YELLOW·BIRDS&·RUBY·PEONIES·
·TOTAL·HEIGHT·24½·  ·FINISH·POLY·GOLD·BLACK&·GREEN·

26    **Figure 38** Original watercolor for design number 7036

HANDEL *Lamps*

· NO· 6925·
· SHADE· 8" DIAM· TEROMA· GLASS·
· ENTIRE· HEIGHT· 14½·
· FINISH· POM· VERDE·

**Figure 39** Original watercolor for design number 6925

Discontinued

ANDEL.

No. 5669.

DIAM. of SHADE 16" - TEROMA GLASS.

HEIGHT 22"

FINISH OLD IVORY.

**Figure 40** Original watercolor for design number 5669

·No· 5698·
· SHADE·16"· TEROMA·
·FINISH· V·A·
·PORTABLE·HEIGHT·24"·

**Figure 41** Original watercolor for design number 5698

No. 5706.
DIAM. of SHADE 16" - TEROMA GLASS.
HEIGHT 22½"
FINISH · V·A·

**Figure 42** Original watercolor for design number 5706

**Figure 43** Original watercolor design for a lamp, executed by Ernest Lewis

**NEW**
*Light*

OUR records show an invariable sales response to every Handel Lamp featured in our advertising. You should take advantage of this fact by having each design displayed prominently in your store at the time it is being advertised in the national magazines.

To make this publicity produce the greatest possible results we shall gladly send you, without charge, envelope stuffers like enclosed sample, with your name imprinted, to send to your best patrons. How many can you effectively use?

Electrotypes for newspaper advertising, as per enclosed proof, will be furnished free.

Remember that all inquiries from prospective customers in your vicinity will be referred to you.

Our publicity with your sales-punch will make this a prosperous Handel season for you.

## THE HANDEL COMPANY
Meriden, Conn.

## NEW LIGHT ON
## HANDEL *Lamps*

THIS circular throws new light on our sales activities in connection with Handel Lamps. They have attained a new pinnacle of popularity. The appeal of the lamps themselves and the push of our advertising are responsible.

But the most vigorous, most extended advertising program of our history begins with May. Quarter-page space will be taken in all the following magazines with the exception of Good Housekeeping, in which somewhat larger space will be used:

| | | |
|---|---|---|
| Country Life in America | Vogue | Harper's Magazine |
| House and Garden | Harper's Bazar | Century |
| House Beautiful | Scribner's Magazine | Good Housekeeping |

On other pages you will find a proof of the May advertisement and a three-color reproduction of the lamp that our May advertising will feature.

To turn this publicity into lamp sales for you, read the last page.

**Figures 44-48** Original 1917 sales brochure, featuring design number 6482

This lamp, 6482, is ready for delivery now.
Price, $30 net. Finish suggested, Matt Copper.
Use the enclosed post card now.

# HANDEL *Lamps*

N̲O matter how simple or elaborate the decorative scheme, there is a Handel Lamp which fits in as an inseparable part of the picture. A distinctive object in a lighted room, this table lamp is a thing of rare beauty, with the light glowing through the browns and yellows of a woodland scene and shining down upon the dull copper standard. A new pattern with all the distinction of Handel craftsmanship.

*Ask your dealer to show you lamp No. 6482 or write for illustrated booklet.*

THE HANDEL COMPANY, 382 East Main Street, Meriden, Conn.

Handel's designers drew their inspiration from a variety of sources, mostly from nature. In addition, they interpreted the styles of the English Arts & Crafts movement, the newly introduced art of Japan and the florid motifs of French romanticism, as expressed in the 'aesthetic' and Art Nouveau tastes. The earliest products of the Company were in the French aesthetic style of painting and this free, naturalistic style in muted palettes remained in popular use throughout the Company's history, especially for the decoration of floral lamp shades. Scenic shades were inspired by real or imaginary landscapes, and some were copied from existing works of art, including old master paintings. During the 1920's, a few designs were introduced of geometric or abstract design in the Art Deco manner.

The content and treatment of a painted shade varied according to the artist responsible for its execution, even in lamps with the same design number, and no two lamps are exactly the same.

Lamp designs and production levels were reviewed by the Company every six months, when designs which showed poor commercial performance were discontinued and new models were introduced into the line. Several dozen new shades could be introduced over the course of a year, in fact, over ninety new designs were put into production during each of the peak years of 1916-1919. In 1915 there were no new designs introduced, due to the death of Philip Handel. Successful designs were often kept in production for several years and it was not uncommon for patterns originally intended for table lamp shades to be reproduced on boudoir shades, floor lamp shades and even on Teroma Art Glass. Slight variations made to the same design over extended periods of production sometimes resulted in the allocation of a new design number.

It is interesting to trace the development of some of the Company's more successful designs, such as the 'Venetian Harbor' pattern, which has a colorful history. The first shade painted with a view of the city of Venice was introduced during the expansive period of the decorating department in 1913, and was one of the several elaborate designs which spearheaded the Company's new lines. The shade was an 18 inch domical and carried design number 5935 (Page 114). In the same year, a 7 inch boudoir shade of conical form was introduced as design number 5925 (Page 188), painted with a similar scene in less detail. Three years later another boudoir shade was introduced as design number 6364 (Page 188), painted with the scene of Venice in finer detail and brighter palette on a domical shade, and a second 18 inch domical shade was marketed in the fall of 1917 as design number 6445 (Page 115). In 1918, Henry Bedigie painted one of the finest shades ever produced by the Company. This 18 inch domical shade, design number 5935/6445 (Page 113), depicts an elaborate panoramic view of the festivities on Ascension Day, known as 'Spazalizio del Mare' ('The Wedding of the City and the Sea'). Another 18 inch shade was introduced in the fall of 1919 as design number 6757 (Page 112), and in this example the boats become the major focal point of the design. Variations of this highly popular design continued to be introduced over a decade of production, the last examples being a 7 inch domical boudoir shade (design number 7168) and a 16 inch domical lamp shade (design number 7135), which were both introduced in 1924.

Another popular shade was decorated with the so-called 'Treasure Island' pattern, designed by Ernest Lewis in 1916 (Page 106) for an 18 inch domical shade and given the design number 6391 (Page 107). The design, which features a sailing vessel entering a moonlit tropical bay, blossomed onto a wide range of Handel products over the next decade, including a 7 inch conical boudoir shade bearing design number 6558 (Page 189), an 18 inch conical shade of multi-pane type bearing design number 6566 (Page 110), and a 10 inch floor lamp shade bearing design number 6574 (Page 208). A pair of these 10 inch shades were also used to accommodate a double arm student lamp base with tulip-shaped sockets (Page 209). All of these examples were available by the fall of 1917. In 1918, an 8½ inch loaf-shaped desk lamp shade was given this design (number 6576) and, in the following year, a version appeared on a 16 inch domical shade as number 6738 (Page 111), but this model does not include the illuminated moon of its predecessors. The final version of the 'Treasure Island' scene to be introduced was on an 8 inch lipped, cylindrical desk lamp shade, featured in the Company's spring advertising campaign of 1922 (Figure 6), bearing design number 6975 (Page 208). The design also appeared on a Teroma Art Glass humidor as design number 4204 (Page 234), dating from 1917.

In the early months of 1919, an 18 inch shade decorated with an allover floral design featuring butterflies, was introduced and extensively advertised in various national publications (Page 160). The domical shade, painted in tones of rose, green, mauve, yellow, brown and orange, against a blue ground shading to purple, bears the identification number 6688 (Page 161). The stylized rose blossoms are usually vividly colored toward the bottom of the shade and soften and grow fainter toward the top, creating the impression of a field of flowers under a summer sky. Because of the popularity of this design, an almost identical shade was introduced in 1922. This 18 inch domical shade was painted in yellow, green and brown tones and is identified as design number 6950 (Page 165). In the fall of 1923, a third 18 inch shade, design number 7032, was made available (Page 164). In this particular example, the rose blossoms and butterflies cover only the lower portion of the shade. From time to time, this basic floral design was introduced into the lamp lines with slight modifications. In the fall of 1919, for example, an 8½ inch loaf-shaped desk lamp shade bearing design number 6760 was produced (Page 210). Other variations include a 7 inch domical boudoir shade (in 1917) bearing design number 6452 (Page 200), and an 'egg' lamp shade (in 1926) identified by design number 7408 (Page 212).

Another successful motif, which was introduced and extensively advertised in the spring of 1921 (Page 128), was produced on an 18 inch shade decorated on the exterior with a sparsely wooded landscape with four colorful birds in flight. The domical shade, painted in tones of green, brown, gray and gold bears design number 6868, and was simultaneously produced in a shade molded with eight vertical lobes. Both shades were available with an internal frosting, giving it either a matte white wash (Page 129), or a blue iridescent wash (Page 130). Variations of this design were introduced in the 1921 fall lamp line in a 10 inch hanging ball pendant with design number 6885, as well as in a 6 inch globe, primarily intended for use as a wall sconce. The 6 inch globe was also available on special order for a unique hanging fixture that featured four to seven globes suspended in varying heights from bronzed metal links attached to an elaborately fashioned ceiling fixture. In 1922, a shade almost identical to design number 6868 was put into production and identified as design number 6953 (Page 131). The difference between the two shades is that the interior of the latter shade was given a gold wash. In the same year, a 7 inch domical boudoir shade with design number 6911, a 10 inch elliptical shaped boudoir shade with design number 6929, torcheres with design number 6991 (Page 214), as well as a davenport lamp, were introduced. Similar designs were also incorporated in a 10 inch Teroma Art Glass vase with design number 4217 (Page 231), and a 9 inch etched vase with design number 4256 (Page 228).

The design and decorating departments formed the nucleus of The Handel Company, but were only part of a well-structured network of small, interdependent units, each of which was essential to the Company's prosperity.

The advertising and sales department, managed by John McGrath during the peak period of production, became increasingly more important during the financially difficult years of the late 1920's. The innovative efforts of its staff were largely responsible for prolonging the Company's existence into the 1930's.

The management and administrative departments were expertly run throughout the Company's history by a succession of Handel family members, who also supplied a consistency in management policy.

Under the foremanship of Patrick Loughran, a separate department existed for chandelier and fixture production. There, ceiling and wall lights of every type were assembled and wired for electricity, many of them designed by Company designers to fit the special requirements of a private or commercial patron. Fixtures for many churches, government and commercial buildings, including St. Rosa's Church and the Polish National Hall in Hartford, were made by this department. With lamp sales on the decline in the late 1920's, the Company actively sought to increase this end of its business and many commercial contracts were fulfilled, including those for hotels in Cleveland, Atlanta and Philadelphia.

Other production departments included a spraying room, supervised by William Clark, where shades and bases were given ground colors from paint guns operated by compressed air, as well as a mold making shop where plaster models of shades were cast, together with all molds for the Company's metalware.

Charles F. Ketelhut, who came from the Edward Miller Company in 1912, was the foreman molder of the casting department and a valuable addition to the Company. He developed a formula for the sand mixture of the molds which resulted in castings with a smooth finish which required very little buffing or polishing. He remained with the Company until his retirement in 1931. A seven-man buffing and polishing department for the final treatment of lamp bases and metalwork was headed by Frank Goda.

# BASES AND METALWORK:

The bases of Handel lamps were as many and varied in design as the shades they supported, and their manufacture was carried out to an equal standard of quality by specialized craftsmen.

Prior to the opening of the Company's foundry, bases and metal fittings were acquired from local manufacturers and suppliers, including the Miller Company, which was the principal source. Many models were commissioned from designs by Philip Handel and George Lockrow.

Under the direction of Antone Teich, bases were made at the Company foundry from 1903. The majority were made in white metal (an alloy of zinc, lead and tin, also known as 'spelter'), using the 'slush molding' technique which was well-suited for high levels of production and the properties of white metal. The process, which is similar to the slip casting method used in ceramics, requires the preparation of metal master molds (usually of bronze or iron) composed of two, three or four segmental sections, depending on the complexity of the design. The white metal is poured in molten (about 850°F) and 'slushed' around to penetrate all areas of the mold. The metal cools on contact with the master mold and, after a few seconds, excess metal is poured out, leaving a covering of semi-molten metal, usually to a thickness of about ¼ inch. When the metal is completely cooled the mold is opened and the casting removed, at which time mold lines and surface flaws are filed to a smooth finish.

The softness of white metal, a function of its high lead content, allowed this form of 'dressing' and any surface repairs to be carried out quickly and easily. At this stage, models without neck-stem risers were completed with soldering and the casting was ready for patination.

The vast majority of Handel metalwork is white metal and, although a few smaller lamp bases were made in spun pewter, bronze was rarely used. Base neck-stems were, however, made of bronze or brass tubing, which was necessary because of the component's small diameter in relation to the weight of the glass shade it supported. On rare occasions bases were made of glass which was usually decorated to match the shade. These glass bases were used exclusively on boudoir lamps (Figure 49).

The base neck-stem was a standard component in the remarkably well-designed and engineered bases made by Handel, which were introduced over the first few years of this century when the electric lamp was still in its infancy. Larger lamps included a cluster ball fitted onto the neck-stem which held two, three or (rarely) four bulb sockets. The cluster ball could be set at any height on the stem by means of threaded pipe extenders,

**Figure 49**  A selection of glass boudoir bases, painted on the exterior. Height: 14 in. (35.5 cm.)

which were made in various lengths. The height was set in relation to the size and shape of the shade, which also determined the number of light bulbs used (18 inch shades normally required three bulbs). The cluster ball sat below a heat cap riser which was available in a number of designs and was normally attached to the stem by means of a bolt finial screwed in from above. Glass shades could be fitted directly onto the heat cap by means of an interlocking ring system designed by Philip Handel and Antone Teich and patented by them in 1910. (Figures 50-55)

**Figure 50** Lamp base components

**Figure 51** A selection of heat caps and finials

**Figure 52** A selection of heat caps and finials

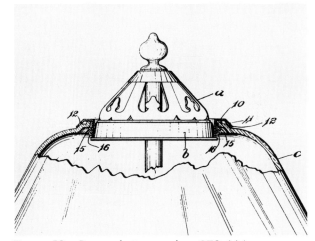

**Figure 53** Patent design number 979,664 for interlocking ring system

**Figure 54** Interlocking ring system

**Figure 55** A selection of pull chains

The engineering skills of Handel and Teich led to a number of ingenious metal lamp fittings, including a multitude of wall and ceiling brackets and a patented screw system for joining metal rimmed panes in multi-panel lamp shades (Figures 56-57).

During the early years of the century it was popular to convert lamps from oil or kerosene to electric power, and lamps containing 'plugged' oil fonts are not uncommon. These should not be confused with oil lamp base designs which were adapted by The Handel Company and made as electric fixtures. As a further confusion, a few models were produced which could function as electric or oil lamps, with the sockets held away from the glass chimney by a cage system (Figure 58).

Boudoir bases were either fitted with a metal harp or with three or four projecting arms which held the shade. This 'spider' system included a rim ring for additional stability in some larger models (Figures 59-61).

**Figure 56** Bolt and lug system for joining metal-rimmed panes

**Figure 57** Bolt and clamp system for joining metal-rimmed panes

**Figure 58** Oil base with cage system

**Figure 59** Boudoir base components

**Figure 60** Boudoir base with 'spider' system

**Figure 61** Base with 'spider' system and rim ring

Handel metalwork drew much of its appeal from the variety of decorative patinas and finishes with which it was treated. The majority of lamp bases made prior to World War I were given a variety of 'bronzed' finishes, which were achieved through several techniques. An 'antique' bronze effect, which Handel termed *Verdegreene* or *Verde Antique*, was achieved by treating the metal with acid which was allowed to eat into the surface for several hours before being washed off, leaving a pitted, greenish finish. All of Handel's metalwork, including 'Verde' finished pieces, were first given a plating of copper in order to prevent a reaction between the base metal and the surface material or atmosphere. This copper finish was sometimes left in a polished state, but normally the metal was patinated in a variety of bronze tones, ranging from almost black *(Ebony)*, to bright and brassy. Patina formulas were jealously guarded by the Handel platers, rather like glaze recipes are by ceramicists, and it is estimated that as many as one hundred may have been used over the Company's period of production. In addition to those previously mentioned, other popular patina's included: *Red Copper, Flemish Brass, Matt Copper, Brush Brass, Sun Verde, Old Ivory, Venetian Brown, English Bronze, Pom. Verde, Gilt Bronze, Antique Gold, Polychrome Gold, Polychrome Gray, Polychrome Silver and Polychrome White.*

After 1916, an increasing number of bases were finished in polychrome enamels (which was done in the decorating shop) or plated with silver or brass. These techniques did not require the metal to be copper plated and were largely introduced because of the wartime shortage of copper.

The Handel foundry specialized in lamp bases, brackets and other components, although a variety of other metal objects were designed and manufactured, including the mounts for 'Handel Ware', door knockers, door stops, the handles for funeral caskets and bookends, which were a favorite product and complemented Handel's library lamps (Figure 62).

**Figure 62**

Mark:       *stitched Handel Lamps tag and relief molded HANDEL*

Height:    *7¼ in. (18.5 cm.)*

A pair of bronze bookends, cast in the form of a panelled door surmounted by an architrave window and framed by pilasters, the base modelled as a flight of three round stone steps.

# CHAPTER III

## HANDEL WARE AND TEROMA ART GLASS

The name Handel is generally associated with decorative lamps, but The Handel Company also produced small decorative objects throughout its history. The earliest evidence of 'ware' production appeared in an advertisement of 1886, and offered "vases, jardinieres, plaques, salts, etc." (Figure 3). Objects of this type, decorated at the old factory, were produced throughout the late 19th century. This early 'reck decorated' ware was in the form of inexpensive items in opal glass with painted (Figure 63) or transfer printed decoration (Page 239, design number 115/280), together with a small amount of hand painted porcelain plates and dishes (Figures 64-65). Under the direction of Albert Parlow, the decorating department gradually expanded the line from opal glass and began to work on more porcelain tableware, which was imported 'blank' from Germany and the Limoges factories in France. The 'outside decoration' of porcelain was relatively common among American workshops in the early 20th century. Many of these workshops, including Handel's, employed their own interpretation of the 'aesthetic' style favored in late 19th century France. A number of Handel decorators specialized in ware, especially the pattern painters who produced table services, tea sets and the like. A few of these artists were allowed to sign their work, including Julius Runge and Walter Wilson, an Englishman who specialized in floral decorated tableware. The Handel painters' earliest efforts on porcelain met with moderate commercial success, although the ware was produced in limited quantity into the 1920's. During World War I, when imports from Europe were restricted, Japanese porcelain was used.

The opal glass and ceramic items decorated at Handel's works fall into two general categories: items of standard design purchased directly from a manufacturer's line, and items designed by The Handel Company, the blanks for which were commissioned from glass and china suppliers.

Among the most popular items of Handel Ware were smokers' articles, introduced in 1908. Unlike the majority of ware decorated prior to this time, the smokers' articles were an exclusive product of The Handel Company. Most of these items were fitted with metal mounts made in the Handel foundry after designs by Philip Handel and Antone Teich, and most examples bear the Company's painted or stamped mark. These humidors, ashtrays,

**Figure 63**

Design number: *none*
Mark: *stamped HANDEL WARE shield*
Height: *6 in. (15 cm.)*

Porcelain character jug with loop handle, modelled as a puckish face in elaborate hat and ruffled collar edged in gilt.

strikers and related articles proved quite popular with tobacconists, who frequently used the less expensive pieces as complimentary promotional items (Figure 66).

**Figure 64**

| Design number: | *none* |
| Mark: | *stamped HANDEL WARE shield* |
| Artist signature: | *Runge* |
| Dimensions: | *11 in. x 4½ in. (28 cm. x 11.5 cm.)* |

Limoges porcelain oval dish with shaped, 'metallic' finished pierced rim, painted with a blossoming branch in shades of green, pink, yellow and white, on a shaded lemon ground.

**Figure 65**

| Design number: | *none* |
| Mark: | *stamped HANDEL WARE shield* |
| Artist signature: | *Runge* |
| Dimensions: | *7 in. x 6½ in. (18 cm. x 16.5 cm.)* |

Limoges porcelain shell-shaped dish with shaped, 'metallic' finished rim painted with a spray of blossoms in shades of orange, brown, yellow and white, on a pale shaded ground.

**Figure 66**   *Verso of ashtray featured on Page 241*

Another example of exclusive Handel ware was a range of art glass, designed and introduced by Albert Parlow in 1906. Parlow's 'Teroma' combined the effects of 'chipped' glass (Figure 67) and enamel painting on decorative vases and humidors in an interpretation of the hand decorated art glass popularized during the 1890's by the Daum Brothers and the School of Nancy in France. The line was relatively unsuccessful in the face of competition from European products and the highly acclaimed art glass of other American manufacturers. Other than examples which were specially commissioned, Teroma Art Glass was discontinued by 1908. In 1917, however, it was reintroduced. This time, pieces of superior quality were executed by the Company's finest decorators. In addition to 'chipped' glass items, a few examples of Handel glassware were made in 'flashed' (applied mineral stain) glass with cut or engraved decoration. These pieces often bear the signature of Palme or Gubisch.

**Figure 67**   Undecorated Teroma Art Glass vase

# CHAPTER IV

## HANDEL MARKS AND DESIGN NUMBERS

Unlike many of its contemporaries, The Handel Company marked the majority of its products. They introduced a consecutive numbering system from its beginning which was applied to lighting fixtures, lamp shades and Teroma Art Glass. These marks provide an invaluable aid in determining the object's date of origin. Handel Ware and Teroma Art Glass marks are illustrated and identified, as follows (Figures 68–77):

**Figure 68** *stamped HANDEL WARE shield*

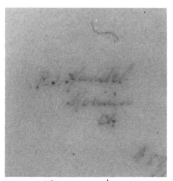

**Figure 69** *painted script signature*

**Figure 70** *painted script signature*

**Figure 71** *stamped HANDEL WARE shield with ribbon*

**Figure 72** *stamped TEROMA seal*

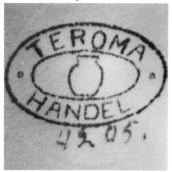

**Figure 73** *stamped TEROMA seal*

**Figure 74** *stamped HANDEL decorator mark*

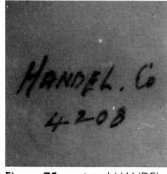

**Figure 75** *painted HANDEL*

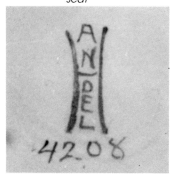

**Figure 76** *painted HANDEL*

**Figure 77** *stamped HANDEL seal*

The majority of lamp bases were signed, usually in molded block letters (either impressed or in relief) and occasionally were incised in script into the molten metal. Most examples were also fitted with a felt pad glued to the bottom of the base, with a stitched fabric tag attached to the felt. Molded or incised numbers are occasionally encountered on bases and these numbers were used by modellers as a design reference. Signature types do not provide a definitive resolution to the date of origin of Handel lamp bases, but many of the bases were modelled in contemporary taste and their period of design can be estimated from this criteria. The most common marks on Handel lamp bases are illustrated, as follows (Figures 78–88):

Figure 78

Figure 79

Figure 80

Figure 81

Figure 82

Figure 83

Figure 84

Figure 85

Figure 86

Figure 87

Figure 88

A design number was also assigned to each base, although this number does not usually appear. The majority of Handel's painted shades were marked with a design number, sometimes accompanied by an artist's signature or monogram (Figure 89). Unlike the marks on bases, Handel Ware or metalwork, shade design numbers can provide useful clues toward the discovery of more information on a particular lamp (including the date of origin, designer, artist and commercial popularity), when cross-referenced with contemporary advertisements, brochures, design sketches and other Handel documentary material.

Figure 89

A study of the lamp shade design numbering system, which is of simple, consecutive, chronological form, reveals a valuable record of the Company's design and production history. The following explanation of the system is derived from the author's research and includes a comparative study of hundreds of actual examples of Handel lamps and other products.

The lowest recorded number on a Handel shade is 41, which appears on an opal glass globe decorated with oak leaves, dating from 1892. This number is part of a consecutive numbering system that reached 1032 in 1898, appearing on a "Gone With The Wind" shade decorated with iris blossoms. Aside from the design number, most shades decorated during this period are also marked "P. J. Handel". For a five year period beginning in 1898, the consecutive numbering system was abandoned, but reintroduced in 1903 beginning with number 1900. The lowest design numbers which occur regularly are between number 2100 and number 3500, and appear on a variety of products including kerosene lamps, chandeliers and sconce shades, opal globes and mushroom-shaped shades (either obverse or reverse painted), i.e. number 2186 (Page 215). Numbers between 1900 and 2100 were reserved for bases and metalware. Designs for bases and metalware were also interspersed among the 5100 to 5400 series of numbers. Many products, including ceiling fixtures, leaded and Teroca lamps, were given a design number that was not included on the finished article. This practice continued throughout the Company's history. The majority of recorded numbers are on painted lamp shades. The table on Page 47 shows the year of introduction of design numbers appearing in this book. It is important to remember that popular designs were often manufactured over a long period of time, sometimes several years, and that design numbers refer only to the date of origin of the design, not necessarily the date in which an object bearing the number was made.

Every number in the consecutive numbering system may not correspond to a finished item, since each sketched or proposed design was allocated a number even though it may not ever have been put into production. Furthermore, runs of numbers were 'skipped' for a variety of reasons and reserved for future use, as in the case of design numbers 3600 to 4000, which were reserved for special commission items, and 4000 to 4500, which were intended for use on Handel Ware (4000 to 4200) and Teroma Art Glass (4200 to 4500). Design numbers for lamp shades begin again with 4900, numbers 4500 to 4900 having never been implemented.

| DESIGN NUMBER | YEAR | PAGE NUMBER | DESIGN NUMBER | YEAR | PAGE NUMBER | DESIGN NUMBER | YEAR | PAGE NUMBER |
|---|---|---|---|---|---|---|---|---|
| 2186 | 1903 | 217 | 6578 | 1917 | 14 | 6959 | 1922 | 132 |
| 2331 | 1916 | 182 | 6586 | 1917 | 92 | 6961 | 1922 | 73 |
| 3410 | 1909 | 216 | 6625 | 1918 | 65 | 6971 | 1922 | 103 |
| 3604 | | 75 | 6632 | 1918 | 148 | 6975 | 1922 | 208 |
| 5484 | 1911 | 74 | 6634 | 1918 | 64 | 6977 | 1922 | 11 |
| 5664 | 1911 | 61 | 6635 | 1918 | 69 | 6989 | 1923 | 13 |
| 5669 | 1911 | 28 | 6636 | 1918 | 57 | 6991 | 1922 | 214 |
| 5698 | 1911 | 29 | 6644 | 1918 | 54 | 6997 | 1922 | 214 |
| 5706 | 1911 | 30 | 6672 | 1919 | 184 | 7007 | 1923 | 13 |
| 5889 | 1912 | 56 | 6675 | 1919 | 205 | 7008 | 1923 | 191 |
| 5895 | 1912 | 215 | 6688 | 1919 | 161 | 7010 | 1923 | 13 |
| 5925 | 1913 | 188 | 6699 | 1919 | 199 | 7011 | 1923 | 194 |
| 5935 | 1913 | 114 | 6704 | 1919 | 192 | 7012 | 1923 | 90 |
| 5946 | 1913 | 70 | 6709 | 1919 | 194 | 7015 | 1922 | 196 |
| 5961 | 1913 | 187 | 6735 | 1919 | 156 | 7021 | 1923 | 145 |
| 6004 | 1913 | 86 | 6738 | 1919 | 111 | 7023 | 1923 | 135 |
| 6068 | 1917 | 14 | 6741 | 1919 | 95 | 7026 | 1923 | 137 |
| 6209 | 1914 | 51 | 6743 | 1919 | 102 | 7028 | 1923 | 134 |
| 6211 | 1914 | 71 | 6749 | 1919 | 101 | 7032 | 1923 | 164 |
| 6212 | 1914 | 88 | 6752 | 1919 | 78 | 7035 | 1923 | 133 |
| 6230 | 1914 | 85 | 6755 | 1919 | 53 | 7036 | 1923 | 26 |
| 6231 | 1914 | 185 | 6757 | 1919 | 112 | 7045 | 1923 | 91 |
| 6236 | 1914 | 207 | 6760 | 1919 | 210 | 7069 | 1923 | 197 |
| 6242 | 1914 | 200 | 6767 | 1920 | 205 | 7073 | 1923 | 126 |
| 6281 | 1914 | 93 | 6778 | 1919 | 14 | 7088 | 1924 | 127 |
| 6310 | 1916 | 92 | 6785 | 1920 | 12 | 7091 | 1924 | 126 |
| 6318 | 1916 | 211 | 6802 | 1920 | 104 | 7093 | 1924 | 212 |
| 6319 | 1916 | 98 | 6807 | 1920 | 120 | 7094 | 1924 | 213 |
| 6324 | 1916 | 59 | 6810 | 1921 | 140 | 7095 | 1924 | 213 |
| 6334 | 1916 | 151 | 6826 | 1920 | 63 | 7105 | 1924 | 152 |
| 6353 | 1916 | 198 | 6829 | 1920 | 172 | 7108 | 1924 | 94 |
| 6354 | 1916 | 201 | 6842 | 1920 | 202 | 7110 | 1924 | 155 |
| 6363 | 1916 | 183 | 6843 | 1920 | 181 | 7115 | 1924 | 62 |
| 6364 | 1916 | 188 | 6846 | 1921 | 140 | 7119 | 1924 | 123 |
| 6367 | 1917 | 14 | 6852 | 1920 | 12 | 7120 | 1924 | 138 |
| 6391 | 1916 | 107 | 6858 | 1921 | 206 | 7121 | 1924 | 167 |
| 6437 | 1917 | 77 | 6868 | 1921 | 129 | 7122 | 1924 | 169 |
| 6445 | 1917 | 115 | 6872 | 1921 | 140 | 7123 | 1924 | 176 |
| 6450 | 1917 | 189 | 6873 | 1921 | 140 | 7128 | 1924 | 139 |
| 6452 | 1917 | 200 | 6874 | 1921 | 141 | 7131 | 1924 | 170 |
| 6455 | 1917 | 183 | 6892 | 1924 | 126 | 7159 | 1924 | 182 |
| 6457 | 1917 | 186 | 6893 | 1921 | 215 | 7160 | 1924 | 192 |
| 6470 | 1917 | 66 | 6894 | 1922 | 11 | 7175 | 1924 | 195 |
| 6482 | 1917 | 33 | 6896 | 1921 | 124 | 7181 | 1924 | 205 |
| 6497 | 1917 | 96 | 6905 | 1922 | 191 | 7183 | 1924 | 206 |
| 6501 | 1917 | 154 | 6907 | 1922 | 190 | 7316 | 1925 | 157 |
| 6516 | 1916 | 196 | 6910 | 1922 | 193 | 7408 | 1926 | 212 |
| 6529 | 1917 | 83 | 6916 | 1922 | 198 | 7423 | 1926 | 76 |
| 6534 | 1917 | 72 | 6918 | 1922 | 199 | 7442 | 1926 | 177 |
| 6536 | 1917 | 67 | 6919 | 1922 | 13 | 7447 | 1926 | 173 |
| 6557 | 1917 | 184 | 6925 | 1922 | 27 | 7452 | 1926 | 97 |
| 6558 | 1917 | 189 | 6926 | 1922 | 11 | 7538 | 1926 | 117 |
| 6563 | 1917 | 186 | 6927 | 1922 | 11 | 7597 | 1926 | 202 |
| 6564 | 1917 | 201 | 6930 | 1922 | 125 | 7645 | 1927 | 216 |
| 6566 | 1917 | 110 | 6931 | 1922 | 11 | 7685 | 1927 | 146 |
| 6572 | 1917 | 210 | 6937 | 1922 | 68 | 7686 | 1927 | 147 |
| 6574 | 1917 | 209 | 6947 | 1922 | 55 | 7816 | 1928 | 171 |
| 6575 | 1917 | 159 | 6950 | 1922 | 165 | 7817 | 1928 | 166 |
| 6577 | 1917 | 207 | 6953 | 1922 | 131 | 7912 | 1930 | 174 |

*Landscapes*

Design number:     *6209*
Artist signature:  *R.*
Diameter:          *18 in. (46 cm.)*

The domical shade in 'chipped', 'sand-finished' glass, painted on the exterior and interior with a densely wooded lakeland landscape in thickly-applied green, and tones of brown and black, against a pale yellow cloudy sky shading to an orange sunset; on bronzed metal baluster base with octagonal vasiform stem and gadrooned and banded stepped circular foot.

*The appearance of viewing deep into a forest through trees is cleverly achieved in this extremely effective design by painting the large foreground trees on the exterior, and smaller trees reflected in the water in the background, with more distant trees painted on the interior.*

*An almost identical domical shade, painted on the exterior and the interior with a lakeside forest scene in shades of green, yellow, orange and brown, bearing design number 6164, was in production in 1911/1912.*

Design number:   *none*
Artist signature:   *E.L.*
Diameter:   *18 in. (46 cm.)*

The conical shade in 'chipped', 'sand-finished' glass, painted on the interior with a scene
of a densely wooded glade with grassy knolls in the foreground and large beech trees in
the background in shades of green, brown, crimson and mauve, the leafage illuminated;
on bronzed metal base of polygonal, dropped-baluster form, the foot molded to simulate
a Chinese carved and pierced hardwood stand.

Design number: *6755*
Artist signature: *R.*
Diameter: *18 in. (46 cm.)*

The domical shade in 'chipped', lightly 'sand-finished' glass, painted on the interior with a landscape including ponds and clumps of deciduous trees in pastel tones of green, brown, pink, blue and yellow, with purple mountains in the distance, under a colorful summer sky of similar palette; on bronzed metal base of baluster form molded with a pattern of Art Nouveau motifs, raised on a cruxiform foot, the upper section molded as a stylized tree trunk.

*The muted pastel effect, in the manner of French Impressionism, is achieved through careful and skilled application of paint over the interior.*

Design number:     6644
Artist signature:   H.B.
Diameter:           18 in. (46 cm.)

The domical shade molded with eight vertical lobes, in 'chipped', lightly 'sand-finished' glass, painted on the interior with a lily pad-dotted stream flowing through a wooded landscape of maple, beech and poplar trees, in mottled tones of green, brown, yellow, russet and crimson, against a cloudy evening sky of yellow, mauve and orange; on bronzed metal base of baluster form, molded with stylized petals ascending the body, raised on circular spreading foot with scalloped border, the upper section molded as a stylized tree trunk.

*The richness of color in this shade is achieved through the heavy application of a variety of colors.*

Design number:   *6947*
Artist signature:   *John Bailey*
Diameter:   *18 in. (46 cm.)*

The domical shade in 'chipped', lightly 'sand-finished' glass, painted on the interior with a densely wooded landscape including birch, oak, and copper beech trees in shades of russet, green, brown, and magenta, against a bright sky shading to gold; on bronzed metal base with single knop, of inverted floriform, molded with petals in low relief.

Design number:   *5889*
Diameter:        *18 in. (46 cm.)*

The conical shade in 'chipped', lightly 'sand-finished' glass, painted on the exterior and interior with a romantic wooded landscape in tones of brown, green, and russet, featuring a rustic track and sketchily-painted trees outlined against a pale sky with pink-edged clouds on the interior; on bronzed metal downward-flaring base of ridged, hexagonal form, molded as a stylized tree trunk.

*Similar stylistically to shade number 6636 (see opposite page), the treatment of the trees, horizon level, and cumulus clouds in this design are reminiscent of the oil sketches of the English romantic landscape artists of the early 19th century.*

Design number:  6636
Diameter:       18 in. (46 cm.)

The domical shade molded with eight vertical lobes, in 'chipped', yellow 'sand-finished' glass, painted on the interior and exterior with a romantic wooded landscape featuring classical ruins in mottled browns, greens, and mauve against a pale blue cloudy sky; on bronzed metal base with urn-form stem molded with a dentil frieze and border of stiff leaves, on square foot.

*The three-dimensional perspective is heightened in this design by painting those elements in the foreground on the interior. The unusual choice of subject is typical of European paintings of the second half of the 18th century.*

Design number 6636; detail

# THE HANDEL COMPANY

MAKERS OF

## HANDEL LAMPS & LIGHTING FIXTURES

FACTORY & OFFICES

### MERIDEN, CONN. MAY 6, 1921.

NEW YORK
200 FIFTH AVE.

2264

TERMS
2198

Sold to  W.J. GEIGER,

GERMANTOWN, PA.

F.O.B. MERIDEN
USUAL PACKAGE CHARGE
NO ALLOWANCE FOR BREAKAGE

| | | | |
|---|---|---|---|
| 1/12 | Dz. 6324 Electrolier M.C. | NO CHARGE | |
| 1 | Tierce #3169 | | |

VIA AMERICAN EXPRESS PREPAID

# THE HANDEL COMPANY

MAKERS OF

## HANDEL LAMPS & LIGHTING FIXTURES

FACTORY & OFFICES

### MERIDEN, CONN.

NEW YORK
200 FIFTH AVE.

Apr. 20, 1921

MR. W. J. GEIGER
C/O THE PHILADELPHIA ELECTRIC CO.
TENTH & CHESTNUT STS.
PHILADELPHIA, PA.

Dear Geiger:-

    If you will give me your house
address, I will have a #6324 lamp sent you
with our compliments.  Best regards.

Very truly yours,

J. A. Roberge

JAR/D
CA

Original correspondence and shipping invoice for lamp number 6324

Design number:   *6324*
Diameter:          *18 in. (46 cm.)*

The domical shade in 'chipped', 'sand-finished' glass, painted on the interior with a continuous wooded lakeland scene featuring birch and poplar trees in shades of pink, green, brown, and blue against a pale gray sky with an illuminated moon; on bronzed metal downward-flaring base of ridged, hexagonal form, molded as a stylized tree trunk.

Design number:    *6324*
Diameter:         *18 in. (46 cm.)*

*Another example of design number 6324, illustrating the variation in composition and coloration which typically occurs in shades which were executed over a period of years by various decorators.*

Design number:    *5664*
Artist signature:  *W. R.*
Diameter:          *18 in. (46 cm.)*

The conical shade in 'chipped', 'sand-finished' glass, painted on the interior with a continuous wooded lakeland scene, featuring birch and poplar trees in shades of pink, green, brown, and blue, against a pale sky with an illuminated moon; on bronzed metal amphora-form base, the top cast with four rib handles, raised on four square, spreading bracket feet.

Design number:   *7115*
Diameter:        *18 in. (46 cm.)*

The domical shade in 'chipped', lightly 'sand-finished' glass, painted on the interior with a sparsely wooded rolling landscape including birch and ash trees in tones of green, brown, gold, and mauve, under a pale gray morning sky shading to lemon yellow, with an illuminated sun casting light onto the water; on bronzed metal base with simple baluster stem and spreading, circular foot.

Design number:    *6826*
Diameter:           *18 in. (46 cm.)*

The domical shade molded with eight vertical lobes, in 'chipped', lightly 'sand-finished' glass, skillfully painted on the interior with a scene of a stream winding through a wooded glade in a palette of green, russet, yellow, brown and pink, the rocks, water, and distant sky illuminated; on bronzed metal base, the bulbous lower section raised on four bracket feet and molded with a forest in low relief, the upper section molded as a stylized tree trunk.

Design number:  *6634*
Diameter:  *18 in. (46 cm.)*

The domical shade in 'chipped', 'sand-finished' glass, painted on the interior with a
sparsely wooded river landscape with clusters of silver birch in the foreground in tones of
green, orange, and gray against a deep pink evening sky streaked with gray clouds; a
muted coral pink coloration is achieved by an allover red wash on the shade interior; on
bronzed metal oviform base molded with a band of stylized flora at the shoulder in the Art
Nouveau taste, raised on four bracket feet, the upper section molded as a stylized tree
trunk.

Design number:   *6625*
Diameter:        *18 in. (46 cm.)*

The domical shade in 'chipped', lightly 'sand-finished' glass, painted on the exterior and interior with a continuous landscape, the foreground with clumps of birch trees and vegetation in thickly-applied green, yellow, and pink enamels, the background painted on the interior, featuring a river and sparse vegetation with mauve and gray rolling hills in the distance, under a pale illuminated sky; on bronzed metal base of broad baluster form, molded with petals in low relief in the Art Nouveau taste, the upper section molded as a stylized tree trunk.

Design number:   *6470*
Diameter:        *18 in. (46 cm.)*

The conical shade in 'chipped', 'sand-finished' glass, composed of six shaped, vertically-ridged panels with scalloped edge, in metal support, painted on the interior with a continuous wooded landscape featuring flora in the foreground and including poplar, maple, and beech trees in shades of green, mauve, brown, yellow, gray, and orange under a bright blue cloudy summer sky; on bronzed metal baluster base molded with leafing trees in low relief, the roots spreading across the circular foot.

Design number:    6536
Diameter:         18 in. (46 cm.)

The domical shade in 'chipped', lightly 'sand-finished' glass, painted on the interior with a continuous band of fern and goldenrod in bright Crystal green, gray and Crystal yellow, and an illuminated butterfly, on a background of radiating pines against a crimson evening sky; on bronzed metal base with urn-form stem molded with a dentil frieze and border of stiff leaves, on square foot.

Design number:   6937
Diameter:        18 in. (46 cm.)

The domical shade in 'chipped', 'sand-finished' glass, painted on the interior with a lakeland landscape featuring two copses of birch trees in shades of green, brown, magenta, and gray, with rolling hills in the background, under a blue sky with pink and white clouds; on bronzed metal base with single knop, of inverted floriform, molded with petals in low relief.

Design number:    *6635*
Diameter:          *18 in. (46 cm.)*

The domical shade in 'chipped' glass, painted on the interior with a continuous birch woodland scene in tones of green and gray against a purple evening sky shading to burnt orange, featuring an illuminated moon reflecting in water; on bronzed metal base of ovoid form, molded with two bands of overlapping petals in relief in the Chinese manner, the foot molded to simulate a Chinese carved and pierced hardwood stand, the upper section molded as a stylized tree trunk.

*The illuminating effect, achieved by eliminating color in an isolated area, is used to dramatic effect in this fine example of an evening scenic shade.*

Design number:   *5946*
Diameter:        *18 in. (46 cm.)*

The conical shade in 'chipped', 'sand-finished' glass, composed of six shaped, vertically-ridged panels with scalloped edge, in metal support, painted on the exterior and interior with a continuous band of trees silhouetted against a crimson and yellow shaded evening sky; on bronzed metal base, the bulbous lower section raised on four bracket feet and molded with a forest in low relief, the upper section molded as a stylized tree trunk.

Design number:    *6211*
Artist signature:   *H.B.*
Diameter:          *18 in. (46 cm.)*

The domical shade in 'chipped', 'sand-finished' glass, skillfully painted on the exterior and interior with a mountain landscape, including two waterfalls, in tones of brown, orange, and green on the interior, the exterior with evergreen and deciduous trees giving perspective, all against a pale blue cloudy sky; on bronzed metal base naturalistically modelled as a gnarled tree trunk, the roots spreading across the circular foot.

Design number: *6534*
Diameter: *18 in. (46 cm.)*

The domical shade molded with eight vertical lobes, in 'chipped', 'sand-finished' glass, painted on the interior with a woodland landscape of birch trees in tones of brown, green, russet, and gray, including a farm building on the horizon, under a pale evening sky streaked with mauve and green and shading to a gray streaked orange sunset.

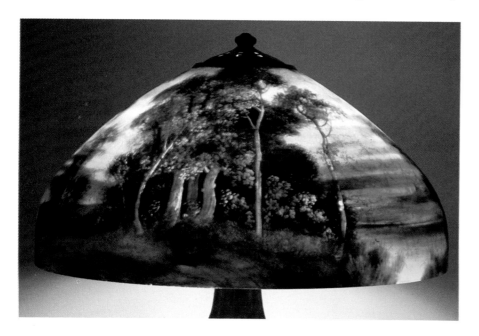

Design number: *6534*
Diameter: *18 in. (46 cm.)*

The domical shade molded with eight vertical lobes, in 'chipped', lightly 'sand-finished' glass, painted on the interior with a continuous wooded landscape of birch trees in tones of green, brown, mauve, and gray, against a mottled sky shading to a crimson sunset.

*These examples of design number 6534 illustrate the variation in composition and coloration often found in shades painted by different artists.*

Design number:    *6961*
Artist signature: *John Bailey*
Diameter:         *16 in. (40.5 cm.)*

The domical shade in 'chipped', lightly 'sand-finished' glass, painted on the interior with a continuous lakeland scene of grasses and water in the foreground, reflecting a copse of trees silhouetted against a sunset of crimson, golden yellow, and mauve; on bronzed metal 'spool-turned' baluster base.

*This base is complete with original pressed glass decorative pulls, which were available in a variety of colors and patterns.*

Design number:    5484
Artist signature:    A. Parlow
Diameter:    18 in. (46 cm.)

The conical shade in 'chipped', yellow 'sand-finished' glass, painted on the exterior and interior with a rustic footbridge in wooded river landscape in tones of predominant green with brown and gray, under a pale sky shading through lemon yellow to a pink sunset; on bronzed metal base with single knop, of inverted floriform, molded with petals in low relief.

*Typical of many shades decorated on both the exterior and interior, the majority of painting on this example is done on the exterior. Only the distant trees and sky details appear on the interior. The entire upper shade is unpainted, giving the sky in this design an illuminated effect.*

Design number:   *3604*
Artist signature:   *J. B.*
Diameter:   *18 in. (46 cm.)*

The conical shade in 'chipped', 'sand-finished' glass, painted on the exterior with a desert scene, featuring a lion and clumps of palm trees in tones of green, brown and gray, the interior painted with a camel caravan and sand shading to lilac dunes in the background, under a lemon desert sky; on bronzed metal base, the vasiform stem patterned with a band of stylized leafage at the shoulder, with gently-ribbed spreading circular foot.

Design number: *7423*
Artist signature: *Palme*
Diameter: *18 in. (46 cm.)*

The funnel-shaped shade composed of four curved glass panels, each acid-etched to form a continuous woodland scene with two medieval huntsmen and a doe amidst stylized foliage including ferns, blackberry briers, and trees, enamelled in golden brown and green with blue and purple fruit, the huntsmen wearing colorful costumes, the whole highlighted with black in the recesses, the shade interior coated in white, forming the ground color; on partially-gilt bronzed metal base in the form of three mythical birds of prey, on a pedestal supporting an orb, capped by a loop finial.

Design number 7423; detail

Design number:    6437
Artist signature:    R.
Diameter:            18 in. (46 cm.)

The domical shade in 'chipped', 'sand-finished' glass, painted on the interior with a desert scene featuring an Arab in white garb and a tethered camel resting beneath date palm trees in tones of sandy-brown, green, mauve, orange, and yellow, with lavender dunes in the background, under a pale orange shaded sky; on bronzed metal oil lamp base of broad baluster form with spreading circular foot, molded with overlapping leafage in vertical relief, the upper section molded as a stylized tree trunk.

*This base retains the original wick fitting and glass chimney.*

Design number 6437; detail

Design number:   *6752*
Diameter:        *18 in. (46 cm.)*

The domical shade in 'chipped', lightly 'sand-finished' glass, skillfully painted on the interior with a mountain stream cascading through a rocky landscape dotted with pines in tones of green, brown, and orange, under a pale yellow evening sky streaked with pink clouds, the whole illuminated and enhanced by a golden iridescent wash on the shade interior; on bronzed metal base naturalistically modelled as a twisted tree trunk, with four branches stemming from the upper section, the roots spreading across the circular foot.

Design number:      *6752*
Artist signature:   *H.B.*
Diameter:           *18 in. (46 cm.)*

*Another example of design number 6752, executed by the artist Henry Bedigie, and painted in a lighter palette, without a wash on the shade interior.*

Original 1917 sales brochure, featuring design number 6529

## FALLING LEAVES
### AND RISING SALES

THE great indoors—more vital to most people than the great outdoors—is here again. Thoughts are turning to new things for the house. There is plenty of money in the country and people are taking advantage of the time to increase the attractiveness of their homes. In fact many of your patrons and possible customers are undoubtedly thinking of buying new lamps. Let's make them think of *Handel* Lamps.

To do our share we're advertising in the October issue of the magazines which were such sales stimulators last spring. A quarter-page advertisement (or larger) will appeal to the women of great taste who read these magazines.

| | | |
|---|---|---|
| House Beautiful | Vogue | Harper's Magazine |
| House & Garden | Harper's Bazar | Good Housekeeping |
| Country Life in America | Century | Scribner's Magazine |

A proof of this October advertisement appears on the next page.

That is what we are doing to make these days of falling leaves also days of rising sales—rising sales for you as well as ourselves.

Original 1917 sales brochure, featuring design number 6529

BIG guns alone can't take a trench. Hand-to-hand combats must follow up the attack. We have two ways of helping you capture the possible sales in your town.

One is to let it be known by newspaper advertising that you carry Handel Lamps. You can have electrotypes per the enclosed proof—free.

The other way is to get copies of the October envelope stuffer in the hands of your patrons. Be sure to have Lamp No. 6529 in stock. If so and you can use a quantity of these leaflets to good advantage, let us know. We shall imprint them with your name. If you haven't this number in stock, order it on the enclosed card. Sign and mail now to insure early delivery.

It's the logical time to get going again. Turn on the current.

### THE HANDEL COMPANY
Meriden, Conn.

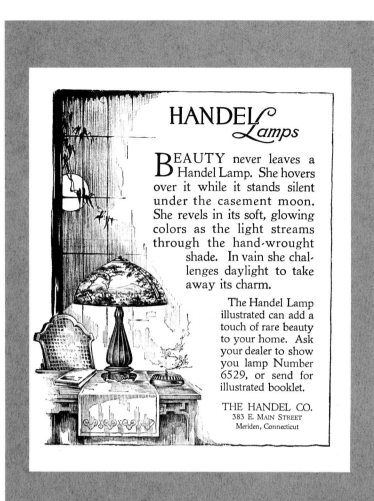

# HANDEL *Lamps*

BEAUTY never leaves a Handel Lamp. She hovers over it while it stands silent under the casement moon. She revels in its soft, glowing colors as the light streams through the hand-wrought shade. In vain she challenges daylight to take away its charm.

The Handel Lamp illustrated can add a touch of rare beauty to your home. Ask your dealer to show you lamp Number 6529, or send for illustrated booklet.

THE HANDEL CO.
383 E. MAIN STREET
Meriden, Connecticut

No. 6529
Height 23½ inches. Diameter of shade, 18 inches
Finish suggested, Ebony.
Price, $27.50
We are prepared to make prompt delivery.

Original 1917 sales brochure, featuring design number 6529

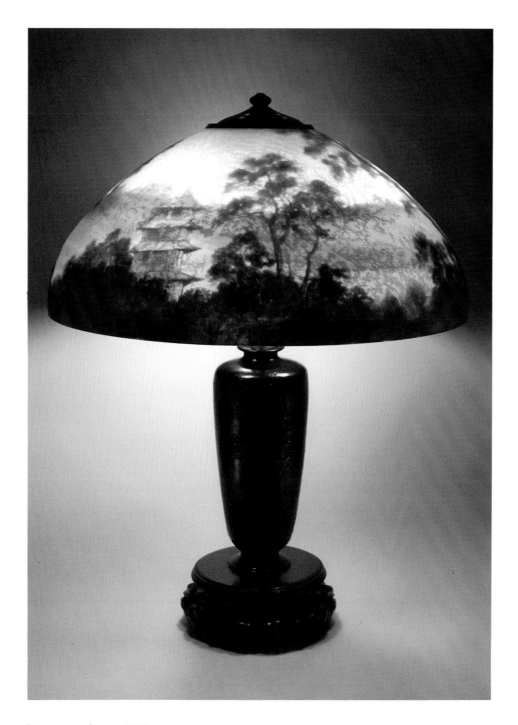

Design number:   *6529*
Diameter:        *18 in. (46 cm*

The domical shade in 'chipped', 'sand-finished' glass, painted on the interior with a pagoda in a sparsely wooded landscape of dominant gray pine trees, in tones of orange and blue under a pale gray sky; on bronzed metal base in the form of a Japanese baluster vase molded with birds and *prunus* blossoms in low relief, the foot molded to simulate a Chinese carved and pierced hardwood stand.

*Several examples of design number 6529 are known to exist, each one slightly different in design composition. For example, this shade features a plain landscape on the verso, while another is painted with a lake dotted with sailing vessels. This variation in shades bearing the same design number is typical of Handel's 'artistic' lamps, which were painted by numerous decorators working from a master design.*

Ad for design number 6230; *Good Housekeeping,* June 1914

Design number:    *6230*
Artist signature:  *W.R.*
Diameter:          *18 in. (46 cm.)*

The domical shade in 'chipped', 'sand-finished' glass, painted on the exterior and interior with a continuous wooded landscape featuring a cluster of silver birch and a road in the foreground, in tones of mottled green, brown, and mauve under a pale blue summer sky dotted with white and pink clouds; on bronzed metal vasiform base molded with vertical ribs in relief, on molded, square foot.

Design number: *6004*
Artist signature: *J.B.*
Diameter: *18 in. (46 cm.)*

The domical shade in 'chipped', 'sand-finished' glass, painted on the interior with a Nile river scene of ruins and an Egyptian village with palm trees in predominant gray with shades of green and tan, under a pale gray morning sky shading to pink, with a yellow rising sun painted on the interior; on bronzed metal base of vertically-ribbed Chinese form, the foot molded to simulate a Chinese carved and pierced hardwood stand, the upper section molded as a stylized tree trunk.

*Design number 6004, though romanticized, depicts the ruins of Elephantine Island, at Aswan in Southern Egypt, showing the famous Nileometer and the Tomb of Omar Khayyam.*

Design number:     *6004*
Artist signature:   *A. Parlow*
Diameter:           *18 in. (46 cm.)*

The domical shade in 'chipped', heavily 'sand-finished' glass, painted on the exterior with a Nile river scene of Egyptian ruins amongst palm trees, in predominant gray with shades of green and mauve, under a pale blue morning sky shading to a lavender sunrise, and an illuminated sun painted on the interior.

*It is interesting to compare this version of the Elephantine Island lamp to the shade on the opposite page, which includes similar elements in a different arrangement and depicts the scene in different light.*

Design number:    *6212*
Artist signature:  *J.B.*
Diameter:          *18 in. (46 cm.)*

The domical shade in 'chipped', 'sand-finished' glass, painted on the interior with a scene of Greek islands with classical ruins in the foreground and a village in the background amongst cypress and olive trees in shades of green, brown, blue, yellow, orange, and purple under a cloudless pale blue summer sky; on bronzed metal base in the form of a ridged, inverted seed pod, raised on scalloped feet, the upper section molded as a stylized tree trunk.

Design number 6212; reverse of shade

Design number:   *7012*
Diameter:          *18 in. (46 cm.)*

The domical shade in 'chipped' glass, painted on the interior with a continuous lakeland wooded landscape in shades of green, yellow, and brown, the foreground of illuminated birch trees against a crimson sunset.

*The rich depth of color in the leafage on this shade is achieved by an unusual variation in thickness in the application of paint.*

Design number:    *7045*
Diameter:            *15 in. (38 cm.)*

The domical shade in 'chipped', 'sand-finished' glass, painted on the interior with a
sparsely wooded landscape, the foreground with dense clumps of illuminated birch trees
in thickly-applied green and brown enamels, against a golden sky shading to a crimson
sunset; on bronzed metal base of slender, squared baluster form with lobed, shaped
square foot.

Design number:   6586
Diameter:         15 in. (38 cm.)

The domed, hexagonal, vertically-ribbed shade in 'chipped', 'sand-finished' glass, painted on the interior with five clumps of palm trees and palm frond undergrowth in shades of green, brown, and charcoal gray against a bright orange sky shading to a crimson sunset, the whole muted with an allover drab olive wash on the interior; on copper finished metal base of ribbed, slender baluster form with ribbed, spreading circular foot cast with a fret design at intervals.

Design number:   6310
Diameter:         15 in. (38 cm.)

The domical shade in 'chipped', 'sand-finished' glass, painted on the interior with clumps of palm trees and palm frond undergrowth in shades of green, brown, and russet, against a low horizon of sand dunes under a golden desert sky; on bronzed metal base of slender, squared baluster form with lobed, shaped square foot, and clear glass ball finial.

Design number:    *6281*
Diameter:         *18 in. (46 cm.)*

The domical shade in 'chipped' glass, painted on the interior with a tropical island scene of dense palms in brown and green tones highlighted in black, against a bright orange sea reflecting distant foliage, under a pale amber sky shading to an orange sunset; on bronzed metal base of Chinese rouleau vase form, incised with a band of fretwork above textured lower section, the foot molded to simulate a Chinese bronze stand.

Design number:   *7108*
Diameter:       *18 in. (46 cm.)*

The conical shade in 'chipped' glass, painted on the interior with a wooded landscape featuring a lake and winding pathway in tones of green, brown, orange, crimson and mauve under a bright blue summer sky with billowing, pink-tinted clouds; on bronzed metal base of inverted lily form.

Design number:   *6741*
Diameter:          *18 in. (46 cm.)*

The conical shade in 'chipped', 'sand-finished' glass, painted on the interior with a moonlit forest scene featuring tall fir trees and a lake in tones of charcoal gray and burnt orange, the streaked sky with an illuminated moon reflected across the water; on bronzed metal base of baluster form, molded with petals and long stemmed buds ascending from the circular spreading foot.

Design number:   *6497*
Diameter:        *14 in. (35.5 cm.)*

The domical shade in 'chipped', 'sand-finished' glass, painted on the interior with a continuous Dutch landscape featuring two windmills, scattered trees and small sea birds in tones of brown and green, leading to a low water horizon, under an evening sky of crimson-edged clouds shaded blue and orange; on bronzed metal base of pear-shaped vasiform, with two flying scroll handles and simple circular foot.

Design number: *7452*
Artist signature: *E.P.*
Diameter: *16 in. (40.5 cm.)*

The domical shade in 'chipped' glass, painted on the interior with a landscape scene featuring a clump of poplars and leafy trees and a flowing stream in the foreground, and rolling hills in the low horizon background, in tones of green, brown, blue, yellow and mauve under a bright lemon sky shading to a coral pink sunrise; on gilt metal base with acanthus finial and barley sugar twist stem with rung terminals, the flat, circular foot with a band of pierced foliate scrollwork.

Design number: *6319*
Artist signature: *John Bailey*
Diameter: *18 in. (46 cm.)*

The domical shade in 'chipped', heavily 'sand-finished' glass, painted on the interior with a continuous woodland scene including elm and ash trees and featuring a grassy cleft, in an autumnal palette of russet and green against a mauve horizon and lemon yellow sky shading to a crimson sunset; on bronzed metal baluster base molded with leafing trees in low relief, the roots spreading across the circular foot.

*Seascapes*

Design number:    *6749*
Diameter:          *18 in. (46 cm.)*

The domical shade molded with eight vertical lobes, in 'chipped', 'sand-finished' glass, painted on the interior with tree-covered islands in shades of green, russet, and brown against a purplish-blue sea with sailboats in the distance, all under a pale gray cloudy sky dotted with sea birds in flight; on bronzed metal base, the bulbous lower section raised on four bracket feet and molded with a forest in low relief, the upper section molded as a stylized tree trunk.

Design number:   *6743*
Artist signature:   *R.*
Diameter:   *18 in. (46 cm.)*

The conical shade in 'chipped', lightly 'sand-finished' glass, painted on the interior with a shorescape featuring clusters of birch trees in mottled shades of green and brown and a stormy sea in ice blue, pink, and white, under a threatening cloudy sky of gray shading through lemon yellow to dusty rose; on bronzed metal base with inverted, floriform stem raised on circular support and six shaped bracket feet.

*The unusual treatment of the waves in this shade may reflect the influence of Japanese art, in particular the woodblock prints of Hokusai.*

Design number: *6971*
Artist signature: *A.*
Diameter: *14 in. (35.5 cm.)*

The domical shade in 'chipped', 'sand-finished' glass, painted on the interior with a scene of a sailing vessel on a golden sea entering a moonlit tropical bay with palm trees and fronds in the foreground, under a purple sky shading to golden yellow, with an illuminated moon casting light across the water; on bronzed metal base with baluster stem and dish foot molded with vertical strapwork and simulated rivet heads in the Arts & Crafts taste.

Design number:    *6802*
Artist signature:    *H.B.*
Diameter:    *15 in. (38 cm.)*

The domical shade in 'chipped', heavily 'sand-finished' glass, painted on the interior with a continuous shorescape featuring a small square-rigged fishing vessel in the foreground, a rocky shoreline and other small boats in the background, in mottled shades of brown and green under a pale blue cloudy sky; on bronzed metal base of pear-shaped vasiform, with two flying scroll handles and simple circular foot.

*The design of this shade is stylistically similar to popular North European paintings of the 19th century and may be an interpretation of an earlier work.*

Design number:   *none*
Artist signature:   *A.P.*
Diameter:   *18 in. (46 cm.)*

The domical shade in 'chipped' glass, painted on the interior with a moonlit seascape including fishing vessels, in predominant russet shading to crimson and highlighted in black, the cloudy sky dotted with sea birds in flight and featuring an illuminated moon reflecting across the water; on patinated metal base with turned baluster stem and circular support raised on four bun feet.

Original pencil sketch, executed in 1916 by Ernest Lewis, and put into production later that year as design number 6391.

Design number:     *6391*
Artist signature:  *A.P.*
Diameter:          *18 in. (46 cm.)*

The domical shade in 'chipped', lightly 'sand-finished' glass, painted on the interior with a scene of a sailing vessel in full sail entering a moonlit tropical bay, the foreground featuring palms in shades of green, mauve, and brown against a shaded blue evening sky with an illuminated moon casting light onto the ship, sea, and clouds; on bronzed metal base with inverted, floriform stem raised on a circular support and six shaped bracket feet.

*This version of shade design number 6391 was painted by Albert Parlow, who was the artistic director of The Handel Company at the time of its manufacture, in 1916. In contrast to the example illustrated on the following page, Parlow's shade is in a softer, brighter palette, bathing the scene in a pallid light evocative of early evening or early morning. Handel's shade colors were carefully chosen to harmonize with the colors and moods of the season of the year in which they were offered for sale. Spring and summer line lamps, from which this example may have been included, tended to be paler and 'cooler' in tone, while fall and winter shades were darker and 'warmer', like Bedigie's version.*

Design number:   *6391*
Artist signature:   *H.B.*
Diameter:   *18 in. (46 cm.)*

The domical shade in 'chipped', lightly 'sand-finished' glass, painted on the interior with a scene of a sailing vessel in full sail entering a moonlit tropical bay, the foreground featuring palms in shades of green, mauve, and brown, against a shaded blue evening sky with an illuminated moon casting light onto the ship, sea, and clouds; on bronzed metal base with inverted, floriform stem raised on a circular support and six shaped bracket feet.

*This is a particularly fine example of a popular shade, painted in this case by Henry Bedigie. The artist has used a dark palette to emphasize the stark, dramatic effect of the 'moon' and illuminated highlights, which are actually areas of the clear glass shade free of any painted decoration.*

Design number 6391 H.B.; detail

Design number: 6566
Diameter: 18 in. (46 cm.)

The conical shade in 'chipped' glass, composed of six shaped, vertically-ridged panels with scalloped edge, in metal support, painted on the interior with a scene of a sailing vessel in full sail entering a moonlit tropical bay flanked by palms, in shades of green, mauve and brown, with a gray-streaked green sea under a shaded violet blue evening sky with an illuminated moon casting light onto the ship, sea, and clouds; on bronzed metal base of baluster form, molded with petals and long stemmed buds ascending from the circular spreading foot.

Design number:   *6738*
Diameter:        *16 in. (40.5 cm.)*

The domical shade in 'chipped', lightly 'sand-finished' glass, painted on the interior with a scene of a vessel sailing over a gray sea into a tropical bay flanked by illuminated palm trees, in tones of brown, green and gray, under a pale evening sky streaked with pink; on bronzed metal base with allover textured finish simulating 'chipped' glass, of slender baluster form with simple, spreading circular foot.

Design number:    *6757*
Artist signature:    *R.*
Diameter:    *18 in. (46 cm.)*

The domical shade in 'chipped', 'sand-finished' glass, painted on the interior with a
Venetian scene with figures in two groups of boats in the foreground and Venice in the
background, San Marco dominant, all in a 'watercolor' palette of pink, mauve, azure
blue, green, yellow and orange tones, the pale blue sky streaked with yellow and mauve
clouds; on bronzed metal baluster form base with everted shoulder, the foot molded to
simulate a Chinese carved and pierced hardwood stand.

Design number:    *5935/6445*
Diameter:          *18 in. (46 cm.)*

The domical shade in 'chipped', lightly 'sand-finished' glass, masterfully painted on the interior with a continuous Venetian scene with figures and boats in sepia tones, on an azure sea, the background depicting San Marco under a cloudy sky of pale blue and streaked purple; on bronzed metal base of baluster form, molded with petals and long stemmed buds ascending from the circular spreading foot.

*This shade depicts the annual festival 'Spazalizio del Mare' ('The Wedding of the City and the Sea'). The palette and style of the painting is typical of contemporary European watercolors.*

Design number 5935/6445; detail

Design number: *5935*
Diameter: *18 in. (46 cm.)*

The domical shade in 'chipped', 'sand-finished' glass, painted on the interior with a Venetian scene, featuring a group of small boats and numerous figures in the immediate foreground, gondolas and Venice in the background, San Marco dominant, in a 'watercolor' palette of pink, mauve, azure blue, green, yellow and orange tones, the pale blue sky streaked with yellow and mauve clouds; on gilt metal base of *Meiping* form with two loose-ring mask handles, the foot molded to simulate a Chinese carved and pierced hardwood stand.

Design number: *6445*
Artist signature: *H.B.*
Diameter: *18 in. (46 cm.)*

The domical shade in 'chipped', 'sand-finished' glass, painted on the interior with a Venetian scene with figures, boats and gondolas in the foreground, Venice in the background, San Marco dominant, in a 'watercolor' palette of pink, mauve, azure blue, green, yellow and orange tones, the pale blue sky streaked with yellow and mauve clouds; on bronzed metal base of ovoid form, molded with two bands of overlapping petals in relief in the Chinese manner, the foot molded to simulate a Chinese carved and pierced hardwood stand, the upper section molded as a stylized tree trunk.

Design number *7538; detail front panel*

Design number 7538; detail rear panel

Design number:     *7538*
Artist signature:   *Bedigie*
Diameter:           *18 in. (46 cm.)*

The shaped, rectangular shade composed of four flat and four curved leaded glass panels, with textured finish on the exterior, the interior skillfully painted with an underwater scene of goldfish swimming amongst aquatic plant life, in a colorful palette of Crystal green, gold, orange, purple, green, blue, yellow and brown enamels, the background in streaked yellow, blue and pink; on bronzed metal figural base in the form of a kneeling mermaid holding a clamshell, with turned metal finial mounted with a Vaseline glass knop.

*The unique texturing on the surface of this shade, achieved by the application of a thick enamel layer which reduces to translucent globules in firing, gives an eerie and realistic quality to this powerful underwater design when the lamp is illuminated.*

Design number 7538; detail side panel

Design number 7538; detail rear panel

Design number:   *7538*
Artist signature:   *Bedigie*
Diameter:   *16 in. (40.5 cm.)*

The shaped, rectangular shade composed of eight flat leaded glass panels in 'chipped', lightly 'sand-finished' glass, skillfully painted on the interior with an underwater scene of tropical fish swimming amongst aquatic plant life, in a colorful palette of crimson, green, orange, yellow, blue, and coral pink, the background streaked in yellow, gray and blue; on bronzed metal base with two fluted, branching arms leading from 'coiled rope' decorated ball knopped baluster stem with trident finial, and spreading foot molded with fish and aquatic vegetation in relief.

Design number:   *6807*
Diameter:          *15 in. (38 cm.)*

The hexagonal, vertically-ribbed shade in 'chipped', 'sand-finished' glass, painted on the interior with an underwater scene of fish swimming amongst aquatic plant life in shades of pink, mauve, orange, yellow and blue; on bronzed metal base with slender baluster stem molded with lily pads, with octagonal foot in the form of an inverted lily pad.

*Birds*

Design number:   *7119*
Diameter:            *18 in. (46 cm.)*

The domical shade in 'chipped', heavily 'sand-finished' glass, painted on the interior with a wave-edge border of stylized exotic birds of paradise and foliate scrollwork in amber, green, red, pink, yellow, and blue on an orange ground, the upper section golden orange; on bronzed metal vasiform base molded with a frieze of stylized leafage, with simple spreading circular foot.

Ad for design number 6930; *Century Magazine,* December 1919

Design number:     *6930*
Artist signature:  *Bedigie*
Diameter:          *18 in. (46 cm.)*

The domical shade in 'chipped', lightly 'sand-finished' glass, painted on the interior with a border patterned with six colorful, stylized exotic birds of paradise amidst stylized rose blossoms, in shaded pink with green and brown foliage on a black ground, beneath a pattern of radiating alternate black and orange stripes on a Crystal yellow ground; on bronzed metal baluster form base, the fluted stem leading from acanthus terminal and ribbed, spreading circular foot.

No. 7088

Pendant
Black and Gold
No. 7091

Boudoir Lamp in
Polychrome Gold
No. 7073

Floor Lamp with
Fabrikon Shade
No. 6892/3426–14"

Torchere
No. 6989

HANDEL LAMPS are noteworthy examples of master craftsmanship. Each is designed and made for permanence, to give life-long service as well as to enhance the attractiveness of the room it adorns. The lamp pictured above illustrates the unusual in decorative treatment, the rare artistry of line and fine balance between shade and standard that make Handel Lamps so distinctive and so desirable.

All Handel shades are painted by hand with colors that are fadeless. All standards and metal parts specially treated to afford a decorative finish as enduring as the metal itself.

Floor lamps, electroliers, pendants, wall sconces, boudoir lamps and torcheres—a few of which are shown—provide a Handel Lamp for every purpose, for every room. They, or other styles and designs, may be purchased at stores of the better sort. Ask to see them. The name Handel is on every lamp.

# HANDEL *Lamps*

Ad for design number 7088; *House & Garden*, June 1924

Design number:    *7088*
Diameter:          *18 in. (46 cm.)*

The domical shade in 'chipped' glass, painted on the exterior with a symmetrical pattern of peacocks centering a floral device in the Art Nouveau manner in golden yellow, blue, green, brown, and pink, the interior painted in mottled Crystal yellow; on bronzed metal base of polygonal, dropped-baluster form, the foot molded to simulate a Chinese carved and pierced hardwood stand.

# HANDEL *Lamps*

*A* CERTAIN beauty of form and exquisite blend of coloring cause one instinctively to associate a Handel Lamp with the fine paintings and beautiful rugs of a perfectly appointed home. And a Handel Lamp is just as lasting also; it is designed to be permanent—different from the fragile lamp that so soon fades and is so easily broken. The lamp shown is No. 6868. Look for it in the stores you visit, or write for the name of nearest dealer.

THE HANDEL COMPANY, MERIDEN, CONN.

Ad for design number 6868; *Century Magazine*, May 1921

Design number:    *6868*
Diameter:          *18 in. (46 cm.)*

The domical shade molded with eight vertical lobes in 'chipped', 'sand-finished' glass, painted on the exterior with a sparsely wooded landscape with four birds in flight in predominantly pale shades of green, brown, yellow, and gray against a frosted matte ivory sky; on bronzed metal base in the form of a Japanese baluster vase molded with birds and *prunus* blossoms in low relief, the foot molded to simulate a Chinese carved and pierced hardwood stand.

*The 'frosting' effect is present on the interior of the shade, helping to accentuate the pale coloration in this version of design number 6868.*

Design number:    *6868*
Diameter:         *18 in. (46 cm.)*

*In this example of design number 6868, produced on a domical shade, the background features a pale blue iridescent sky.*

Design number:   *6953*
Diameter:        *18 in. (46 cm.)*

The domical shade in 'chipped' glass, painted on the exterior with a sparsely wooded landscape with three birds in flight in shades of green, brown, gray, orange and gold, against an iridescent melon-colored sky streaked with gold; on bronzed metal base in the form of a Japanese baluster vase molded with birds and *prunus* blossoms in low relief, with gadrooned and banded stepped circular foot.

Design number:   *6959*
Diameter:   *16 in. (40.5 cm.)*

The domical shade in 'chipped', lightly 'sand-finished' glass, painted on the interior with a scene of ducks flanked by trees and foliage in the foreground, flying over a mangrove swamp in shades of russet, mauve and golden yellow, under a pale sky shading to yellow and pink; on bronzed metal globular base with two scroll handles, raised on simple circular plinth.

Design number:    *7035*
Diameter:         *18 in. (46 cm.)*

The domical shade in 'chipped', lightly 'sand-finished' glass, painted on the interior with three colorful parrots and butterflies amidst blooming branches in predominant pale green, highlighted with mauve and illuminated, on a dark green ground; on polychromed metal base with leaf-clad orb finial and baluster stem molded with long stemmed daisies and acanthus leaves, the circular foot molded with an acanthus border.

Design number:      7028
Artist signature:   *Broggi*
Diameter:           *18 in. (46 cm.)*

The domical shade molded with eight vertical lobes, in 'chipped', lightly 'sand-finished' glass, painted on the interior with two colorful parrots perched on branches laden with wild rose blossoms in shades of pink with yellow stamens and green leafage, including a large butterfly, with a background of bold charcoal gray pine trees silhouetted against a turquoise sky; on polychromed metal vasiform base, the molded relief painted in the Japanese manner with birds in flight and blossoming flora in green and gilt, on gadrooned and banded stepped circular foot, all on an ivory ground.

Design number 7028; detail

Design number:   *7023*
Diameter:          *18 in. (46 cm.)*

The domical shade in 'chipped', lightly 'sand-finished' glass, painted on the interior with a pair of colorful parrots and a large butterfly amidst branches of blossoming peonies, the petals in shaded rose and yellow, the foliage in tan, all against a charcoal gray matte ground; on bronzed metal base with leaf-clad baluster stem, raised on four foliate supports and square, petal-molded foot in the Art Nouveau taste.

*DURING* the long, bleak evenings of winter, the soft, colorful beauty of a Handel Lamp adds a warm glow of friendly welcome to every room. So skillfully are the rich colors blended that there is a perfect harmony between shade and standard—between lamp and the most thoughtfully selected interior draperies and furnishings.

The true beauty of permanence is wrought into each Handel Lamp. With ordinary care, it will last for a lifetime.

You will find many exquisite designs at the better dealers—one which blends with your decorative plan in every room.

The name "Handel" is on every genuine Handel Lamp. Look for it when you select the lamp for your home or for a distinctive gift. The table lamp illustrated is No. 7026.

*The newest Handel creations for the living-room are the graceful mantel lamps fashioned after the rarest of Colonial models. Three of the most distinctive designs are illustrated. You may see them at the better dealers.*

# HANDEL *Lamps*

Ad for design number 7026; *House Beautiful*, November 1923

Design number:   7026
Diameter:        18 in. (46 cm.)

The domical shade in 'chipped', lightly 'sand-finished' glass, painted on the interior with two pair of colorful stylized exotic birds of paradise amidst stylized blossom-laden branches in shades of blue and salmon highlighted in Crystal lime green, all on a black matte ground; on bronzed metal base with leaf-clad scrolling tripod support, with gadrooned and banded stepped circular foot.

Design number 7026; detail

Design number:     *7120*
Artist signature:   *Walter*
Diameter:           *18 in. (46 cm.)*

The domical shade in 'chipped', lightly 'sand-finished' glass, painted on the interior with two pair of colorful stylized birds of paradise amidst berry-laden blossoming branches in tones of bright Crystal blue, green, brown and yellow, all on a mottled dusty pink ground; on bronzed metal base of vertically-ribbed Chinese form, the foot molded to simulate a Chinese carved and pierced hardwood stand, the upper section molded as a stylized tree trunk.

Design number:    *7128*
Artist signature:    *Palme*
Diameter:    *18 in. (46 cm.)*

The domical shade in 'chipped', 'sand-finished' glass, painted on the interior with three colorful parrots perched on branches of *prunus* blossoms with petals of shaded rose and Crystal yellow ochre and green leafage, all on a marbleized white ground with veins of pink, violet, gray, green, and blue Crystal; on bronzed metal base of polygonal, dropped-baluster form, the foot molded to simulate a Chinese carved and pierced hardwood stand.

6810

6858

6873

6846

6872

*140 Birds*

HEITLAND

Above Lamp
No. 6874

THE delight derived from the cool furnishings and cheerful cretonnes and chintzes of the summer home is one that is greatly enhanced by the bright glow of a Handel lamp. Beauty of color, grace of line and unrivalled skill in workmanship are the characteristics which place Handel lamps in the homes where good taste is everywhere evident.

The satisfying variety from which to select enables one to choose a lamp without which the gleam of that mahogany desk, the comfort of a deep-cushioned chair, or the secluded intimacy of the boudoir would be incomplete. And the permanence of Handel lamps assures their becoming a lasting part of the home. The lamps shown here may be purchased at your dealer's. There is a Handel lamp for every corner.

THE HANDEL COMPANY, 120 E. Main Street, Meriden, Conn.

# HANDEL *Lamps*

Ad for design number 6874; *House Beautiful*, June 1921

Design number:     *6874*
Artist signature:  *Broggi*
Diameter:          *18 in. (46 cm.)*

The domical shade in 'chipped', lightly 'sand-finished' glass, skillfully painted on the interior with three colorful scarlet macaws, two perched and one in flight, amidst tropical foliage in shades of green, gold, pink, brown, and blue; on polychromed metal vasiform base, the molded relief painted in the Japanese manner with birds in flight and blossoming flora in green and gilt, on gadrooned and banded stepped circular foot, all on an ivory ground.

*The illuminating effect, achieved by eliminating color in an isolated area, is used to dramatic effect on the eyes of the birds.*

Design number:     6874
Artist signature:   R.
Diameter:              18 in. (46 cm.)

Another example of design number 6874, featuring reverse of shade.

Design number:    *6874*
Artist signature:    *Palme*
Diameter:    *18 in. (46 cm.)*

*Another example of design number 6874, executed by the artist George Palme, painted in a lighter palette.*

HANDEL LAMPS add the richness, the soft, colorful beauty so desirable in a well-planned room. Each Handel Lamp is a graceful tone poem in color, as well as an unsurpassed lighting fixture. The standards are designed to harmonize with the exquisite, hand-painted shades. *The Handel Lamp illustrated is No. 7021.* You will find it, together with other Handel designs, at the better class of stores. The name "Handel" on every lamp is a definite guarantee of satisfaction.

# HANDEL *Lamps*

THE HANDEL COMPANY - - MERIDEN, CONN.

Ad for design number 7021; *Scribner's*, November 1923

Design number:     *7021*
Artist signature:   *A.P.*
Diameter:           *18 in. (46 cm.)*

The domical shade in 'chipped,' lightly 'sand-finished' glass, painted on the interior with two colorful exotic birds of paradise in flight against a black ground patterned with areas of stylized leafage in mottled orange, and clusters of Oriental blossoms with white and pale blue petals and Crystal yellow stamens and leafage; on polychromed metal base with leaf-clad finial and baluster stem molded with long stemmed daisies and acanthus leaves, the circular foot molded with an acanthus border.

*The treatment of the ground in this shade shows the comtemporary influence and taste for Japonisme.*

Design number:    *7685*
Artist signature:  *Mosher*
Diameter:         *18 in. (46 cm.)*

The domical shade in 'chipped', 'sand-finished' glass, painted on the interior with two colorful stylized exotic birds of paradise amidst tropical foliage in tones of brown, pale green, pink, and black on a lime green ground; on bronzed metal base in the form of a Japanese baluster vase molded with *prunus* blossoms and birds in low relief, with gadrooned and banded stepped circular foot.

Design number:  *7686*
Diameter:        *18 in. (46 cm.)*

The funnel-shaped shade composed of four curved glass panels, two etched with a design of a parrot in flight amidst tall grasses, two etched with a similar grass design, enamelled in ochre, the parrots brightly enamelled, all on a gray streaked frosted ground; on gilt metal base with double scroll finial, ball-knopped baluster stem and dish base, raised on four scroll feet.

Design number:    6632
Diameter:         18 in. (46 cm.)

The conical shade in 'chipped', 'sand-finished' glass, painted on the interior with a continuous seascape depicting sea birds highlighted with illumination flying over a pale gray sky; on bronzed metal base with inverted floriform stem raised on a circular support and six shaped bracket feet.

# *Flowers*

Design number:   *6334*
Diameter:         *15 in. (38 cm.)*

The domed, hexagonal, vertically-ribbed shade in 'chipped', 'sand-finished' glass, painted on the interior with a border of budding and blossoming roses with pink petals, yellow stamens, and green leafage, with four predominantly Crystal yellow butterflies hovering above, and on the exterior with floral sprigs picked out in green enamel, all against a pale ground shading to golden yellow at the crown; on bronzed metal base with double scroll finial and fluted stem of inverted trumpet form, on molded circular foot.

Design number:    *7105*
Diameter:          *18 in. (46 cm.)*

The domical shade in 'chipped' glass, painted on the interior with a band of blooming roses with shaded pink illuminated petals and green and brown leafage, against a mottled Crystal yellow ground; on gilt metal base with elaborately-turned double baluster stem over a 'drip-pan' and molded, square foot in the Renaissance Revival taste.

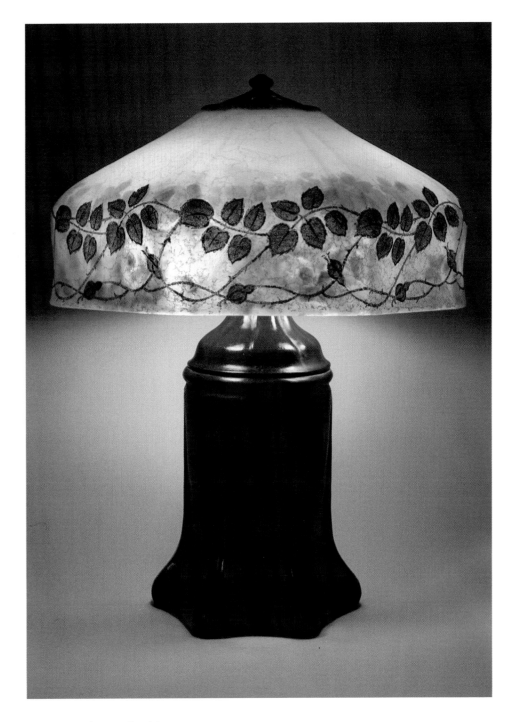

Design number:    *illegible*
Diameter:         *18 in. (46 cm.)*

The octagonal, vertically-ribbed shade with dropped apron in 'chipped', 'sand-finished' glass, painted on the interior with a border of blooming roses in muted tones of pink, lime green, and brown, and on the exterior with a continuous meandering rose brier in dark green, all on a golden yellow ground; on bronzed metal base of cylindrical, downward-flaring form, molded with six vertical ribs in relief, the upper section molded as a stylized tree trunk.

Design number: *6501*
Diameter: *15 in. (38 cm.)*

The bell form shade in 'chipped', heavily 'sand-finished' glass, painted on the interior with a band of Crystal yellow goldenrod with Crystal green leafage and violet and blue-petalled wildflowers with yellow stamens, on a pale blue ground shading to dusty pink at the rim; on bronzed metal base with fluted, slender oviform stem and circular spreading foot molded with radiating ribs.

Design number: *7110*
Artist signature: *Rochette*
Diameter: *18 in. (46 cm.)*

The conical shade in 'chipped', lightly 'sand-finished' glass, painted on the interior with an allover pattern of overlapping leafage in an autumnal palette of russet, yellow, green, and gray tones against pale yellow; on bronzed metal base of inverted lily form.

Design number:   *6735*
Diameter:        *16 in. (40.5 cm.)*

The molded shade with dropped apron in 'chipped' glass, painted on the interior with a border of meandering blackberry briers, the leafage in green and magenta, the berries in purple and red, the blossoms yellow and illuminated, all on a yellow ground; on gilt metal baluster form base, the surface textured to simulate 'chipped' glass, with spreading circular foot.

*This design is unusual in that it was also available on an 18 inch diameter shade (bearing the same design number).*

Design number:  *7316*
Diameter:       *15 in. (38 cm.)*

The domical shade in 'chipped', lightly 'sand-finished' glass, painted on the interior with stylized berry-laden branches in bright pink, Crystal yellow, and pale green, on a black ground patterned with ice blue 'moons'; on bronzed metal base of slender, squared baluster form with lobed, shaped square foot.

*The bright coloration and stylization shows the influence of Japanese color woodblock prints in the design, which is in sharp contrast to earlier subdued patterns.*

Design number:   *illegible*
Diameter:        *16 in. (40.5 cm.)*

The domed, hexagonal, vertically-ribbed shade in 'chipped', 'sand-finished' glass, painted on the interior with a pond of white water lilies and bulrushes ascending the ribs in the foreground, in tones of brown, green, yellow, and gray shading to a golden orange sky in the distance; on bronzed metal base of cylindrical, downward-flaring form, molded with six vertical ribs in relief, the upper section molded as a stylized tree trunk.

Design number:  *6575*
Diameter:       *18 in. (46 cm.)*

The conical shade in 'chipped', 'sand-finished' glass, painted on the interior with a pond of white water lilies, the foreground featuring bulrushes in tones of green and brown, the background with distant purple trees silhouetted against a pale sky shading to mauve and lavender; on bronzed metal base of cylindrical, downward-flaring form, molded with six vertical ribs in relief, the upper section molded as a stylized tree trunk.

Ad for design number 6688; *Scribner's*, May 1919

Design number:   *6688*
Diameter:        *18 in. (46 cm.)*

The domical shade in 'chipped', lightly 'sand-finished' glass, painted on the interior with an allover pattern of stylized rose blossoms against shaded blue, in predominant deep rose and shades of green, mauve, yellow, brown and orange, with four butterflies in Crystal yellow; on bronzed metal base with leaf-clad scrolling tripod support, with gadrooned and banded stepped circular foot.

Design number:    *6688*
Diameter:            *18 in. (46 cm.)*

The domical shade in 'chipped', lightly 'sand-finished' glass, painted on the interior with an allover pattern of stylized rose blossoms against shaded blue, in predominant pale rose and shades of green, mauve, yellow, brown and orange, with four butterflies in Crystal yellow.

Design number:    *6688*
Diameter:         *18 in. (46 cm.)*

The domical shade in 'chipped', 'sand-finished' glass, painted on the interior with an allover pattern of stylized rose blossoms, in predominant bright rose and shades of green, mauve and brown, with three pale yellow butterflies.

Design number: *7032*
Diameter: *18 in. (46 cm.)*

The domical shade in 'chipped', 'sand-finished' glass, painted on the interior with a border of stylized rose blossoms in muted tones of pink, green, and orange, and three Crystal yellow butterflies, on a lemon yellow ground shading to green, violet and orange; on bronzed metal base with reeded stem and bottle-shaped support molded with a band of stylized waves in the Art Nouveau taste, with four vertical straps descending the body and continuing to form the four feet.

Design number:   *6950*
Diameter:        *18 in. (46 cm.)*

The domical shade in 'chipped', lightly 'sand-finished' glass, painted on the interior with an allover pattern of stylized rose blossoms in a predominantly green palette of lemon yellow, green, and brown tones, with four bright purple butterflies; on bronzed metal base with leaf-clad knop raised on tripod support with anthemion scroll feet, mounted on a gadrooned circular plinth.

*The impressionistic, muted treatment of the flora in this shade is achieved with an allover coating of wash on the interior, only the butterflies are illuminated and isolated.*

Design number:     *7817*
Artist signature:  *Mosher*
Diameter:          *18 in. (46 cm.)*

The domical shade in 'chipped', lightly 'sand-finished' glass, painted on the interior with clusters of wild rose blossoms, the petals in shaded rose and mauve, the stamens Crystal yellow, on branches of green and purple leafage, with four butterflies in Crystal yellow, all on a matte buff ground; on bronzed metal base naturalistically modelled as a gnarled tree trunk, the roots spreading across the circular foot.

Design number: *7121*
Diameter: *18 in. (46 cm.)*

The domical shade in 'chipped', 'sand-finished' glass, painted on the interior with ascending hollyhocks and wildflowers, the petals in shaded blue, purple, and Crystal yellow, the leafage green, against a pattern of muted pink and lavender wild roses, all on a soft pink ground; on bronzed metal base with leaf-clad finial, raised on tripod support with anthemion scroll feet, mounted on a molded white-veined marble circular plinth.

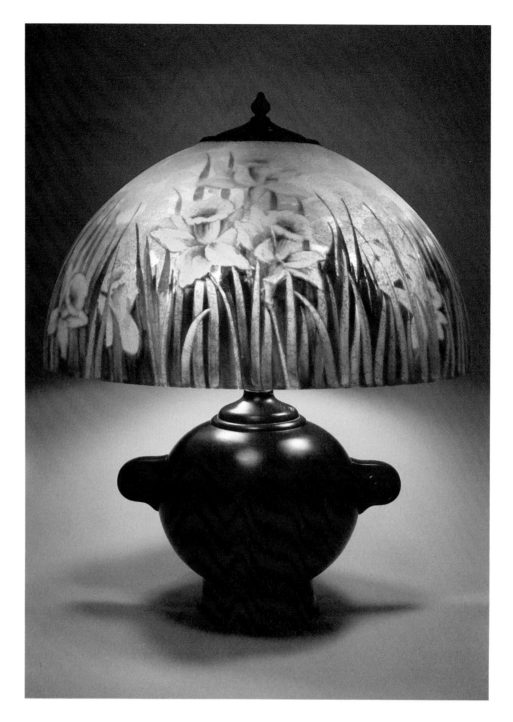

Design number:  *illegible*
Diameter:       *15 in. (38 cm.)*

The domical shade in 'chipped', lightly 'sand-finished' glass, boldly painted on the interior with a continuous band of long stemmed daffodils in the foreground, the petals in golden yellow tones, the leafage grayish-green shading to black, all silhouetted against a pale gray cloudy sky shading to purple; on bronzed metal globular base with two scroll handles, raised on simple circular plinth.

Design number:    *7122*
Artist signature:  *A.P.*
Diameter:          *18 in. (46 cm.)*

The domical shade in 'chipped', 'sand-finished' glass, painted on the interior with a continuous pattern of yellow daffodils and crimson-petalled flowers with yellow stamens on a ground of black, cornflower blue, and pale gray stylized foliage, silhouetted against a pale green sky; on bronzed metal base with leaf-clad orb finial and urn form stem molded with a frieze of stylized leafage, on stepped circular foot in the Neo-Classical taste.

Design number:    *7131*
Artist signature:    *Palme*
Diameter:    *16 in. (40.5 cm.)*

The domical, molded shade in 'chipped' glass, painted on the interior with a continuous band of flowering long stemmed poppies in shades of red with green leafage, buds, and stamens, against an ochre ground; on bronzed metal base with baluster stem and dish foot molded with vertical strapwork and simulated rivet heads in the Arts & Crafts taste.

*An unusual feature of this shade is a floral border and vertical ribs in mold-blown relief, which do not conform to the interior painted decoration.*

Design number:    *7816*
Diameter:          *18 in. (46 cm.)*

The conical shade with notched rim, in 'chipped', 'sand-finished' glass, realistically painted on the interior with a cluster of blooming poppies and dog daisies, with three butterflies, in tones of orange, pink, green, brown, blue, yellow, and white on a pale green shaded ground at the crown; on bronzed metal base in the form of a Japanese vase molded with birds and *prunus* blossoms in low relief, the foot molded to simulate a Chinese carved and pierced hardwood stand.

Design number:     6829
Artist signature:  Bedigie
Diameter:          18 in. (46 cm.)

The conical shade in 'chipped', 'sand-finished' glass, painted on the interior with a continuous band of foliage including ferns, goldenrod, and violet chrysanthemums, with three butterflies, in a palette of greens, browns, and yellows against a blue, cloudy sky shading to mauve; on bronzed metal base with leaf-clad knop raised on tripod support with anthemion scroll feet, mounted on a gadrooned circular foot.

*In this attractive example the floral border forms the only decoration on the shade. A shade with this pattern (design number 6438, not pictured), and similar border patterns, were available painted with landscapes in the background, the border forming an effective foreground and enhancing perspective.*

Design number:  *7447*
Diameter:  *18 in. (46 cm.)*

The domical shade in 'chipped', 'sand-finished' glass, painted on the interior with a continuous band of chrysanthemums, goldenrod and grasses, with three butterflies, in a palette of yellow, green and brown, under a pale sky shading to deep purple; on bronzed metal base of broad baluster form, molded with petals in low relief in the Art Nouveau taste, the upper section molded as a stylized tree trunk.

Design number: *7912*
Artist signature: *Parlow*
Diameter: *18 in. (46 cm.)*

The domical shade in 'chipped', heavily 'sand-finished' glass, painted on the interior with an allover pattern of blooming chrysanthemums in tones of yellow, gold, pink, green, brown, and purple; on bronzed metal base molded in the form of a kneeling classical maiden holding an amphora aloft, with molded octagonal plinth.

*Together with the lamp illustrated on the opposite page, this is another excellent example of a unique shade, painted in this case by Albert Parlow.*

Design number:   *none*
Diameter:        *18 in. (46 cm.)*

The conical shade in 'chipped', 'sand-finished' glass, painted on the interior with an allover pattern of chrysanthemums in the 'aesthetic' style, in shades of pink, green, yellow, gold and blue; on bronzed metal figural base in the form of a kneeling mermaid holding a clamshell.

*This unique shade was painted by the artist in free style and is distinct from the shades produced in the decorating workshops, which were designed for duplicate manufacture and were numbered. Typical of allover floral shades painted in the 'aesthetic' style, the characteristic denser pattern at the lower rim and paler, blue-tinted ground above, gives a naturalistic outdoor effect.*

Design number:    *7123*
Artist signature:    *M.*
Diameter:            *18 in. (46 cm.)*

The domical shade in 'chipped', lightly 'sand-finished' glass, painted on the interior with chrysanthemum blossoms and leafage in shades of green, yellow, pink, orange and mauve, against a lemon ground with a broad band of black and pale blue at the rim; on bronzed metal base in the form of a Japanese baluster vase molded with birds and *prunus* blossoms in low relief, the foot molded to   simulate a Chinese carved and pierced hardwood stand.

Design number:     *7442*
Artist signature:  *Palme*
Diameter:          *18 in. (46 cm.)*

The funnel-shaped shade composed of four curved glass panels, each etched in a pattern of stylized flower heads on a streaked ground in the Japanese taste, enamelled in purple, yellow, white, and salmon pink on a lime green ground; on bronzed metal base with loop finial and triple 'candle' sockets on everted 'drip-pan', raised on turned stem and tripod support with scroll feet, mounted on *antico verde* marble plinth, all in the Renaissance Revival taste.

*The design of this shade effectively exploits the etching and enamelling technique introduced to The Handel Company by George Palme and illustrates the taste for Oriental art during the early 1920's.*

*Boudoirs*

Design number:    *6843*
Artist signature:   *F.*
Diameter:            *7 in. (18 cm.)*

The domical shade in 'chipped' glass, skillfully painted on the interior with a landscape scene featuring tall birch trees and a flowing stream in tones of green, brown, blue, orange, mauve, and lavender, under a pale blue sky; on bronzed metal base, the vasiform stem molded with a dense forest scene in low relief, raised on reel-turned support and four bracket feet.

Design number:    7159
Artist signature:    D.M.
Diameter:    7 in. (18 cm.)

The domical shade in 'chipped' glass, painted on the interior with a sparsely wooded landscape featuring a cluster of vegetation, including pine trees in the foreground in tones of green and brown, with purple rolling hills in the background, under a pale sky streaked with golden clouds; on bronzed metal base naturalistically modelled as a gnarled tree trunk, the roots spreading across the circular foot.

Design number:    2331
Diameter:    7 in. (18 cm.)

The ribbed, domical shade with square, scalloped rim in 'chipped', heavily 'sand-finished' glass, painted on the interior with a continuous landscape featuring a cluster of trees in each corner in shades of pink, green, yellow and orange against an ivory sky; on bronzed metal base of slender, downward-flaring form with reeded stem and circular, dish foot.

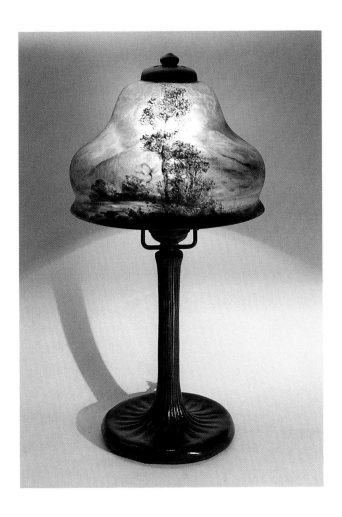

Design number:   6455
Diameter:        7 in. (18 cm.)

The bell-shaped shade with flaring rim in 'chipped', 'sand-finished' glass, painted on the interior with a mountain landscape of pink and blue snow-capped peaks rising above a lake and crimson trees, the exterior foreground of scattered trees in brown and green enamels, all against an ice blue cloudy sky; on bronzed metal base of slender, downward-flaring form with reeded stem and circular, dish foot.

Design number:   6363
Diameter:        7 in. (18 cm.)

The conical shade in 'chipped', lightly 'sand-finished' glass, painted on the interior with a landscape, including birch and cypress trees in the foreground and a farmhouse in the background, in tones of green, brown, pink and gray, all under a pink evening sky with an illuminated moon; on bronzed metal base with swelling stem and spreading circular foot molded with an allover woven strapwork pattern.

Design number:  *6557*
Diameter:       *7 in. (18 cm.)*

The domical shade in 'chipped', 'sand-finished' glass, painted on the interior with a desert scene of a camel caravan silhouetted against a golden orange horizon, the immediate foreground painted with grasses to enhance perspective; on gilt metal base, the vasiform stem molded with a dense forest scene in low relief, raised on reel-turned support and four bracket feet.

Design number:  *6672*
Diameter:       *10 in. (25.5 cm.)*

The elliptical shade in 'chipped', 'sand-finished' glass, painted on the interior with a lakeland landscape dotted with poplar and birch trees in shades of green, mauve, yellow, and brown against a mottled pale pink sky with an illuminated moon; on silvered metal 'candlestick' base with slender, dropped-baluster stem and molded oval dish foot.

Design number:   *illegible*
Diameter:        *7 in. (18 cm.)*

The domical shade in 'chipped', lightly 'sand-finished' glass, painted on the interior with a continuous landscape dotted with trees in green, brown, orange, white, and mauve, against a yellow sky shading to an orange sunset; on bronzed metal downward-flaring base of ridged, hexagonal form, modelled as a stylized tree trunk.

Design number:     *6231*
Artist signature:  *H.H.*
Diameter:          *7 in. (18 cm.)*

The bell-shaped shade with flaring rim in 'chipped', heavily 'sand-finished' glass, painted on the exterior with an impressionistic landscape scattered with vegetation in thickly-applied green, brown, and orange enamels, the interior painted with distant purple hills and a yellow and green shaded sky; on bronzed metal base of slender, baluster form with spreading circular foot, incised with radiating notches.

Design number: *6457*
Artist signature: *A.*
Diameter: *8 in. (20 cm.)*

The ribbed, domical shade with square, scalloped rim in 'chipped', lightly 'sand-finished' glass, painted on the interior with a border of goldenrod and grasses in yellow, green, and brown with two butterflies and mauve mountains in the background, under a pale sky; on bronzed metal base, the vasiform stem molded with a dense forest scene in low relief, raised on reel-turned support and four bracket feet.

Design number: *6563*
Diameter: *8 in. (20 cm.)*

The domed, hexagonal shade with zig-zag rim in 'chipped' glass, painted on the interior with a tropical island scene featuring palm trees, fronds, and vegetation in the foreground in shades of green, brown, crimson and pale blue, and a distant sailing vessel, all under an ice blue sky streaked with crimson clouds and featuring a pale yellow moon; on bronzed metal base, the vasiform stem molded with a dense forest scene in low relief, raised on reel-turned support and four bracket feet.

Design number:    *illegible*
Diameter:         *8 in. (20 cm.)*

The ribbed, domical shade with closed top and square, scalloped rim, in 'chipped' glass, painted on the interior with a winter landscape of bare trees on a carpet of snow silhouetted against a shaded golden amber sky; the shade held by a 'spider' mount on bronzed metal base naturalistically modelled as a gnarled tree trunk, the roots spreading across the circular foot.

Design number:    *5961*
Diameter:         *7 in. (18 cm.)*

The domical shade in 'chipped' glass, painted on the exterior with a winter landscape scene of bare trees on a carpet of snow, with orange and green vegetation in the background, under a clear frosted sky; on bronzed metal base naturalistically modelled as a gnarled tree trunk, the roots spreading across the circular foot.

Design number:   *6364*
Artist signature:   *R.*
Diameter:   *7 in. (18 cm.)*

The domical shade in 'chipped', lightly 'sand-finished' glass, skillfully painted on the interior with a Venetian scene in a 'watercolor' palette, depicting sailing vessels in the foreground and Venice in the background, San Marco dominant, all under a pale green cloudy sky shading to mauve; on bronzed metal base, the slender, dropped-baluster stem raised on fluted terminal and gadrooned, circular foot.

Design number:   *5925*
Diameter:   *7 in. (18 cm.)*

The conical shade in 'chipped' glass, painted on the interior with a Venetian scene in a 'watercolor' palette, featuring sailing vessels and a gondola in the foreground, Venice in the background, San Marco dominant, under a pale blue and yellow sky shading to pink with an illuminated moon; on bronzed metal base with reeded, columnar stem raised on acanthus terminal and leaf-molded circular foot.

Design number:  *6450*
Diameter:  *7 in. (18 cm.)*

The conical shade in 'chipped', lightly 'sand-finished' glass, painted on the interior with a moonlit harbor scene featuring numerous boats in sepia tones, under a burnt orange sky with an illuminated moon visible through clouds; on bronzed metal base with reeded, columnar stem raised on acanthus terminal and leaf-molded circular foot.

Design number:  *6558*
Diameter:  *7 in. (18 cm.)*

The conical shade in 'chipped', 'sand-finished' glass, painted on the interior with a scene of a sailing vessel in full sail entering a tropical bay dotted with palm trees, in pale gray, brown, and sea green, under a pale gray sky with an illuminated moon shedding light onto the ship, sea, and clouds; on bronzed metal base of ribbed, baluster form with molded quatrefoil foot.

Design number: *6907*
Artist signature: *Palme*
Diameter: *7 in. (18 cm.)*

The domed, hexagonal shade with zig-zag rim in 'chipped', heavily 'sand-finished' glass, painted on the interior with a pair of colorful scarlet macaws perched in branches of exotic tropical foliage in tones of green, pink, orange, and mauve against a lemon mottled ground; on bronzed metal base in the form of a Japanese baluster vase , the foot molded to simulate a Chinese carved and pierced hardwood stand.

Design number: *6905*
Diameter: *7 in. (18 cm.)*

The domical shade in 'chipped', lightly 'sand-finished' glass, painted on the interior with three colorful parakeets amongst blossom-laden branches in pink, green, and yellow on a matte black ground; on gilt metal downward-flaring base of ridged, hexagonal form, modelled as a stylized tree trunk.

Design number: *7008*
Artist signature: *E.L.*
Diameter: *7 in. (18 cm.)*

The domical shade in 'chipped', lightly 'sand-finished' glass, painted on the interior with three colorful parakeets perched on blossom-laden branches in Crystal green, pink, yellow, orange and mauve on a lime green ground; on bronzed metal base with fluted columnar stem raised on bud terminal, the foot molded to simulate a Chinese carved and pierced hardwood stand.

Design number:    6704
Artist signature:   K.W.
Diameter:    7 in. (18 cm.)

The hexagonal, panelled shade with dropped apron in 'chipped' glass, painted on the interior with a radiating trellis pattern entwined with wildflowers with pink petals, yellow stamens, and gray leafage on a pale shaded yellow ground; on bronzed metal base with swelling stem and circular foot molded with an allover basket weave pattern.

Design number:    7160
Artist signature:   Palme
Diameter:    7 in. (18 cm.)

The domical shade in 'chipped' glass, painted on the interior with a continuous band of trees, the violet and black trunks silhouetted against a shaded pink sky, the blossoming foliage in tones of black, green, orange and Crystal yellow growing denser at the crown; on bronzed metal base with swelling stem and spreading circular foot, molded with an allover woven strapwork pattern highlighted in red enamel.

Design number:   *illegible*
Diameter:        *7 in. (18 cm.)*

The domical shade in 'chipped', 'sand-finished' glass, painted on the interior with an allover pattern of leaves and branches in an autumnal palette of brown and green against a golden amber ground; on bronzed metal downward-flaring base of ridged, hexagonal form, modelled as a stylized tree trunk.

Design number:   *6910*
Diameter:        *7 in. (18 cm.)*

The bell-shaped shade with flared rim in 'chipped', 'sand-finished' glass, painted on the interior with illuminated apple blossoms and berry-laden branches in shades of green, brown, pink, purple, yellow, and white against a blue-gray ground shading to pale; on bronzed metal base of slender, downward-flaring form with reeded stem and circular, dish foot.

Design number:   *7011*
Diameter:        *8 in. (20 cm.)*

The domical shade with inverted rim in 'chipped', 'sand-finished' glass, painted on the interior with clusters of wildflowers and two butterflies in pale blue and Crystal yellow, against a pattern of stylized leafage in black and red on a pink ground; on bronzed metal base in the form of a Japanese baluster vase, the foot molded to simulate a Chinese carved and pierced hardwood stand.

Design number:   *6709*
Diameter:        *7 in. (18 cm.)*

The hexagonal, panelled shade with dropped apron, in 'chipped', 'sand-finished' glass, painted on the interior with wisteria descending from the crown in tones of pink and green on a pale green ground; on bronzed metal base with swelling stem and spreading circular foot, molded with an allover strapwork pattern highlighted in red enamel.

Design number:    *7175*
Diameter:         *10 in. (25.5 cm.)*

The domical shade in 'chipped', 'sand-finished' glass, painted on the interior with an allover pattern of pansies on a ground of illuminated morning-glories in yellow, cornflower blue, and Crystal green; on bronzed metal base with dropped-baluster stem, the foot molded to simulate a Chinese carved and pierced hardwood stand.

Design number:    *illegible*
Diameter:         *7 in. (18 cm.)*

The domical shade in 'chipped' glass, painted on the exterior with a border of meandering yellow-petalled flowers and mauve-petalled florets, with green leafage and a pattern of descending stylized flower stalks in alternating yellow and orange on a clear frosted ground; on bronzed metal base of ribbed, baluster form with molded quatrefoil foot.

Design number:    6516
Diameter:         7 in. (18 cm.)

The domed, hexagonal, vertically-ribbed shade in 'chipped' glass, painted on the interior with blossoming Japanese quince branches and three butterflies in Crystal yellow, brown, mauve, pink, gray, and blue on a clear frosted ground shading to yellow at the rim; on bronzed metal base of inverted lily form.

*The choice of blossoming Japanese quince and other prunus blossoms reflects the contemporary taste for Japonisme and Oriental art, which experienced a revival in American decorative art in the 1920's.*

Design number:    7015
Artist signature: R.G.
Diameter:         7 in. (18 cm.)

The domical shade in 'chipped' glass, painted on the interior with blossoming Japanese quince branches and three butterflies in Crystal yellow, pink, gray, and blue on a shaded lemon yellow and lime green ground; on bronzed metal base with swelling stem and spreading circular foot, molded with an allover woven strapwork pattern.

*This design was originally introduced in 1916 on a domed, hexagonal, vertically-ribbed shade. The design was reintroduced in 1922 with no obvious differences, however, the design was changed to number 7015. Interestingly, the later design was produced in both a domical and a domed, hexagonal, vertically-ribbed shade.*

Design number:    *7069*
Artist signature:  *E.D.*
Diameter:          *7 in. (18 cm.)*

The domical shade in 'chipped' glass, boldly painted on the interior with a pattern of violet-petalled illuminated pansies, long stemmed poppy heads, and orange-petalled wildflowers with green and gray leafage, against a lemon yellow ground; on bronzed metal base of slender, baluster form with spreading circular foot, molded with a pattern of descending leafage in shallow relief.

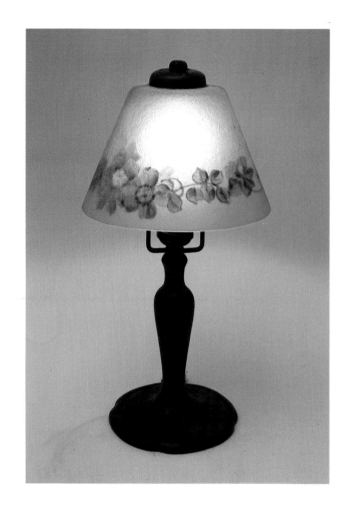

Design number:  *6916*
Diameter:       *7 in. (18 cm.)*

The conical shade in 'chipped' glass, painted on the interior with a border of meandering wild roses, the petals in shaded pink, the stamens yellow, the leafage green and brown, on a pale illuminated ground shading to gold at the lower rim; on bronzed metal base of ribbed, baluster form with molded quatrefoil foot.

Design number:  *6353*
Diameter:       *7 in. (18 cm.)*

The domical shade molded in a basket weave pattern, painted on the interior with a border of wild roses, the petals pink, the stamens yellow, the leafage inky blue and green against a clear frosted ground; on bronzed metal base with swelling stem and spreading circular foot, molded with an allover woven strapwork pattern highlighted in red enamel.

Design number:    *6699*
Diameter:         *7 in. (18 cm.)*

The domical shade in 'chipped', lightly 'sand-finished' glass, painted on the interior with clusters of tea roses with pink illuminated petals and gray leafage on a pale ground; on bronzed metal baluster base molded with leafing trees in low relief, the roots spreading across the circular foot.

Design number:    *6918*
Artist signature: *F.L.*
Diameter:         *7 in. (18 cm.)*

The vertically-ribbed, domical shade in 'chipped', lightly 'sand-finished' glass, painted on the interior with a border of meandering roses and wildflowers, in tones of pink and green on a pale blue-gray ground; on metal base with fluted columnar stem raised on bud terminal, the foot molded to simulate a Chinese carved and pierced hardwood stand, enamelled in gray with pink highlights to complement the shade coloration.

Design number:   6242
Artist signature:   A.H.
Diameter:   7 in. (18 cm.)

The domed, hexagonal, vertically-ribbed shade in 'chipped', 'sand-finished' glass, painted on the interior with scattered wild roses and colorful butterflies in pink, orange, blue, green, and black on a clear, frosted ground; on bronzed metal base with swelling stem and spreading circular foot, molded with an allover woven strapwork pattern highlighted in red enamel.

Design number:   6452
Diameter:   7 in. (18 cm.)

The domical shade in 'chipped', 'sand-finished' glass, painted on the interior with an allover pattern of wild roses, the petals shaded pink and illuminated, the stamens yellow, the leafage green and brown, on a mottled pale green ground; on bronzed metal baluster base molded with leafing trees in low relief, the roots spreading across the circular foot.

Design number: 6564
Artist signature: K.C.
Diameter: 7 in. (18 cm.)

The vertically-ribbed, domical shade in 'chipped', lightly 'sand-finished' glass, painted on the interior with a pattern of meandering wild roses with pink petals, green and white stalks and leafage, on a clear frosted ground; on ivory enamelled metal base with slender, dropped-baluster stem and foot molded to simulate a Chinese carved and pierced hardwood stand.

Design number: 6354
Diameter: 7 in. (18 cm.)

The domed, hexagonal, vertically-ribbed shade in 'chipped', 'sand-finished' glass, painted on the interior with a border of blooming and budding wild roses in shades of pink, orange, and green and with floral sprays in green on the exterior, against a shaded lemon ground; on bronzed metal base of slender baluster form with spreading circular foot, incised with radiating notches.

Design number: *6842*
Diameter: *8 in. (20 cm.)*

The ribbed, domical shade with square, scalloped rim in 'chipped', lightly 'sand-finished' glass, painted on the interior with a repeating floral arrangement stylized in the period taste in pink, green, brown, yellow, orange and black, on a shaded orange ground; on bronzed metal base of slender, baluster form with spreading circular foot, molded with a pattern of descending leafage in shallow relief.

Design number: *7597*
Diameter: *8 in. (20 cm.)*

The ribbed, domical shade with square, scalloped rim in 'chipped', heavily 'sand-finished' glass, strikingly painted on the interior with a repeating geometric Art Deco design in orange, lime green, black, pink, and blue, on a white frosted ground; on gilt metal base with turned finial, turned stem and marbleized knop, on square, shaped bracket foot.

Desk/Piano Lamps
& Miscellany

Design number:   *7181*
Diameter:        *8 in. (20 cm.)*

The lipped, cylindrical shade in 'chipped' glass, painted on the exterior with a symmetrical pattern of two peacocks and leafing branches in green, orange, and blue on a golden yellow ground; pivoted on gilt metal base with adjustable arm and lozenge-shaped spreading foot.

Design number:    *6767*
Artist signature: *F.*
Diameter:         *8 in. (20 cm.)*

The lipped, cylindrical shade in 'chipped' glass, painted on the exterior with a border of elaborate, scrolling foliage centering an urn in buff on a charcoal gray ground, against a mottled orange interior ground; pivoted on bronzed metal base with adjustable arm and molded shoe-form foot.

Design number:    *6675*
Artist signature: *G.D.*
Diameter:         *8 in. (20 cm.)*

The lipped, cylindrical shade in 'chipped' opal glass, painted on the exterior with a band of cornucopae and leaf scrolls in brown, green, orange and blue, reserved against mottled yellow; pivoted on bronzed metal base with adjustable arm and spreading circular foot molded with a blind fret border.

Design number:   *6858*
Diameter:        *8 in. (20 cm.)*

The lipped, cylindrical shade in 'chipped' opal glass, painted on the exterior with an allover landscape scene of trees reflected in a lake and silhouetted against a moonlit sky in shades of green and mauve; pivoted on bronzed metal base with adjustable arm and spreading circular foot patterned with a border of radiating acanthus leaves.

Design number:   *7183*
Diameter:        *8 in. (20 cm.)*

The lipped, cylindrical shade in 'chipped' glass, painted on the interior with a landscape of fir trees flanking a lake and distant mountains in tones of green, brown, and mauve under a shaded golden sky; pivoted on gilt metal base with adjustable arm and molded shoe-form foot.

Ad for design number 6577; *Good Housekeeping*, November 1917

Design number:    *6577*
Diameter:          *8 in. (20 cm.)*

The lipped, cylindrical shade in 'chipped' glass, painted on the interior with a wooded landscape scene with trees in the foreground in tones of brown, silhouetted against an amber sky with an illuminated moon; pivoted on bronzed metal base with adjustable arm and molded shoe-form foot.

Design number:    *6236*
Diameter:          *8 in. (20 cm.)*

The lipped, cylindrical shade in 'chipped' glass, painted on the interior with trees in landscape in shades of green, brown, and mauve under a pale shaded sky; pivoted on bronzed metal base with adjustable arm and molded shoe-form foot.

Design number: *6975*
Diameter: *8 in. (20 cm.)*

The lipped, cylindrical shade in 'chipped' glass, painted on the interior with a scene of a sailing vessel in full sail entering a moonlit tropical bay dotted with palm trees, in shades of green, brown and blue-gray, under a pale gray sky with an illuminated moon passing light onto the ship, clouds, and sea; pivoted on bronzed metal base with adjustable arm and lozenge-shaped spreading foot patterned with a border of leafage.

Design number: *6574*
Diameter: *10 in. (25.5 cm.)*
Overall height: *57 in. (145 cm.)*

The domical shade in 'chipped', lightly 'sand-finished' glass, painted on the interior with a scene of a sailing vessel in full sail entering a moonlit tropical bay dotted with palm trees, in shades of green, brown and blue-gray under a pale gray sky with an illuminated moon passing light onto the ship, clouds, and sea; suspended in bronzed metal harp frame with tulip-shaped socket, raised on a plain standard with bud terminal and stepped, spreading circular foot.

Design number:    6574
Diameter:         10 in. (25.5 cm.)
Overall height:   24 in. (61 cm.)

The domical shades in 'chipped', lightly 'sand-finished' glass, painted on the interior with a scene of a sailing vessel in full sail entering a moonlit tropical bay dotted with palm trees, in shades of green, brown and blue-gray, under a pale blue sky with an illuminated moon passing light onto the ship, clouds and sea; on bronzed metal double arm student lamp base with tulip-shaped sockets, on slender baluster stem and spreading foot molded with scrolled strapwork in low relief.

Design number:    6760
Diameter:         8½ in. (21.5 cm.)

The loaf-shaped shade in 'chipped', lightly 'sand-finished' glass, painted on the interior with an allover pattern of stylized wild roses and leafage in tones of pink, orange, green, yellow and purple, against a shaded and illuminated pale green ground; swung on bronzed metal bridge base with ribbed stem and quatrefoil foot.

Design number:    6572
Diameter:         8½ in. (21.5 cm.)

The loaf-shaped shade in 'chipped', 'sand-finished' glass, painted on the interior with a wooded landscape in tones of brown and green, the trees silhouetted against a pale green illuminated sky streaked with mauve and yellow clouds; swung on gilt metal bridge base with baluster stem and leaf-clad oval dish foot.

Design number:  *6318*
Diameter:        *8½ in. (21.5 cm.)*

The loaf-shaped shade in 'chipped' glass, painted on the interior with a river landscape dotted with birch trees in shades of green and brown, under a pale olive sky shading to an illuminated sunrise; swung on bronzed metal bridge base with ribbed stem and quatrefoil foot.

Design number:   *7408*
Overall height:   *7½ in. (19 cm.)*

The oviform shade in 'frosted' crackle glass, painted on the exterior with a bouquet of colorful stylized wild roses in pink, blue, yellow, green and mauve; on metal base molded to simulate a Chinese carved and pierced hardwood stand, finished in ivory enamel, with original dimmer mechanism adjustable to dim, medium, and bright.

Design number:   *7093*
Overall height:   *7½ in. (19 cm.)*

The oviform shade in 'frosted' crackle glass, painted on the exterior with sprays of stylized wild roses and leafage in dusty rose, cornflower blue, bright green and yellow, the interior with an allover robin's egg blue wash; on metal base molded to simulate a Chinese carved and pierced hardwood stand, finished in ivory enamel, with original dimmer mechanism adjustable to dim, medium, and bright.

Design number:    7094
Artist signature:    R.G.
Overall height:    7½ in. (19 cm.)

The oviform shades in 'frosted' crackle glass, painted on the exterior with a pattern of floral garlands in cornflower blue, green, orange, yellow and brown against a clear, frosted ground; each on metal base molded to simulate a Chinese carved and pierced hardwood stand, finished in brown enamel, with original dimmer mechanism adjustable to dim, medium, and bright.

Design number:    7095
Artist signature:    V.N.
Overall height:    7½ in. (19 cm.)

The oviform shade in 'frosted' crackle glass, painted on the exterior with a pattern of two yellow-plumed stylized parrots and stylized floral sprays in pink, brown, blue and Crystal green, the interior with an allover golden yellow wash; on metal base molded to simulate a Chinese carved and pierced hardwood stand, finished in ivory enamel, with original dimmer mechanism adjustable to dim, medium, and bright.

Design number:    6997
Diameter:         11 in. (28 cm.)

The mushroom-shaped shade in 'chipped' glass, painted on the exterior with two pair of colorful, stylized exotic birds of paradise amidst blossoming branches in tones of russet and green, the interior painted with bold details and with an allover iridescent wash; on bronzed metal hanging stem with petal-molded ceiling plaque and 'tassel' finial.

Design number:    6991
Artist signature: F. Gubisch
Height:           15½ in. (39.5 cm.)

A pair of gilt metal mounted torcheres, the cylindrical shades in 'chipped', lightly 'sand-finished' glass, painted on the exterior with a continuous wooded scene, including birds in flight in green, brown, and black against a shaded yellow ground, the interiors with an allover iridescent wash; the metal covers with acanthus finials, the baluster stemmed bases with spreading circular feet and gadrooned borders.

Design number:    *5895/0389*
Height:    *11 in. (28 cm.)*

The inverted, bell-shaped shade in 'chipped' glass, painted on the exterior with a sparsely wooded landscape, featuring birch trees in the foreground in shades of brown and pastel green, against a shaded golden yellow sky; on bronzed metal base in the form of a chamber candlestick, raised on four bracket feet.

Design number:    *6893*
Diameter:    *10 in. (25.5 cm.)*
Overall height:    *57 in. (145 cm.)*

The domical shade in 'chipped', 'sand-finished' glass, painted on the interior with a lakeland landscape with clumps of trees in the foreground in green, black, and pink, and crimson trees in the background silhouetted against a golden orange sunset; suspended in bronzed metal harp frame with tulip-shaped socket, raised on a plain standard with bud terminal and stepped, spreading circular foot.

Ad for design number 6893; *Atlantic Monthly*, November 1921

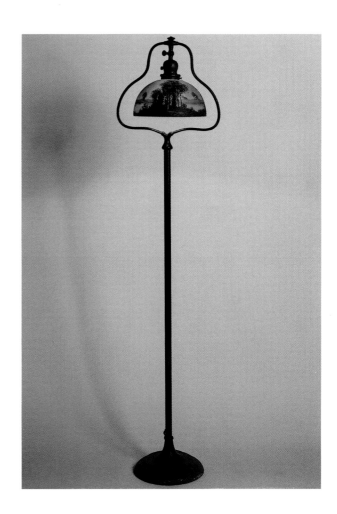

Ad for design number 3410; *The Craftsman,*
August 1913

*These shades were used to accommodate various
types of lighting fixtures.*

Design number:  *3410*
Diameter:  *4 in. (10 cm.)*
Overall height:  *20¾ in. (53 cm.)*

The cylindrical shades in 'chipped' glass, molded to simulate a strapwork armature and rivet heads in the Arts & Crafts taste, enamelled in yellow ochre; on gilt metal double arm student lamp base with tulip-shaped sockets and downward-spreading, circular foot molded with simulated applied strapwork.

Design number:  *7645*
Diameter:  *9 in. (23 cm.)*

The demi-lune shaped shade composed of three leaded glass panels, the front and rear panels etched in a sunburst design enamelled in golden yellow relief against a translucent frosted ground; on gilt metal ball knopped turned stem, with dish base raised on bun feet.

Design number: ˙ *2186*
Artist signature: *Godwin*
Diameter: *10 in. (25.5 cm.)*

The mushroom shade, painted on the interior with a coiled Chinese dragon in Crystal yellow, orange, green, and white enamels, chasing an illuminated flaming pearl on a ground of green swirls, the design including scattered stylized clouds picked out on the exterior in black and gilt; on bronzed metal baluster base with spreading foot applied with 'coiled rope' decoration.

Teroma Art Glass

Design number:   *none*
Mark:   *none*
Artist signature:   *A. Parlow*
Height:   *9 in. (23 cm.)*

Humidor in 'chipped' glass, the interior polished, masterfully painted on the exterior with a pair of mallard in flight over reeds in a landscape dotted with blossoming trees and poplars in tones of green, brown, pink, white, yellow, blue and mauve, on a frosted ground, the lid in 'chipped', frosted glass.

*This is a particularly fine example of the work of Albert Parlow, who headed the production department at the time of its manufacture, circa 1919. The study of the pair of mallard is realistically and painstakingly executed, and was probably taken from an ornithological print. Parlow has successfully created a spring landscape with a careful and skillful application of colored enamels often built up in several layers. The extraordinary detail and lack of design number on this humidor suggest that it is a unique piece, probably produced to a special order.*

Design number:    *4221*
Mark:             *stamped TEROMA seal*
Artist signature: *Bedigie*
Height:           *10 in. (25.5 cm.)*

Vase of cylindrical form with flared rim in 'chipped', 'sand-finished' glass, the interior frosted, painted on the exterior with an Alpine scene of cypress trees and a lake in the foreground with a village beneath snow-capped peaks in the background, in dark shades of green, purple, tan, pink, and yellow under a frosted sky shaded yellow on the rim interior.

Design number:    *4218*
Mark:             *painted HANDEL monogram*
Artist signature: *Bailey*
Height:           *10 in. (25.5 cm.)*

Vase of footed baluster form in 'chipped', 'sand-finished' glass, the interior polished, painted on the exterior with an Alpine scene of cypress and birch trees and a lake in the foreground and snow-capped peaks in the background, in shades of green, tan, yellow, pink and purple against a frosted ground.

Design number: *4209*
Mark: *stamped TEROMA seal*
Artist signature: *F. Gubisch*
Height: *10 in. (25.5 cm.)*

Vase of baluster form in 'chipped', 'sand-finished' glass, the interior frosted, painted on the exterior with a landscape scene including trees reflected in a lake, in tones of green, mauve, yellow and blue on a frosted ground.

Design number:    *4207*
Mark:             *stamped TEROMA seal*
Artist signature: *Broggi*
Height:           *10 in. (25.5 cm.)*

Vase of baluster form in 'chipped' glass, the interior polished, painted on the exterior with a wooded landscape of birch trees in the foreground in shades of green, brown, mauve, and white against a pale lemon yellow sky shading to a dusty pink sunset.

Design number:    *4210*
Mark:             *stamped TEROMA seal*
Artist signature: *Bedigie*
Height:           *10 in. (25.5 cm.)*

Vase of baluster form in 'chipped', 'sand-finished' glass, the interior polished, painted on the exterior with a landscape scene of birch and fir trees in the foreground in shades of green, tan, and mauve, and purple hills in the background, under a frosted sky.

Design number:     *4214*
Mark:              *stamped TEROMA seal*
Artist signature:  *Loehner*
Height:            *10¾ in. (27.5 cm.)*

Vase of footed floriform with ruffled rim in 'chipped', 'sand-finished' glass, the interior polished, painted on the exterior with a pattern of palm trees ascending from the foot in shades of brown, tan, green, and gray against a frosted ground.

Design number:     *4220*
Mark:              *stamped TEROMA seal*
Artist signature:  *Gubisch*
Height:            *8½ in. (21.5 cm.)*

Vase of shouldered, baluster form in 'chipped', 'sand-finished' glass, the interior frosted, painted on the exterior with a low horizon landscape and birch trees in shades of green, yellow, and orange against a mottled blue sky shading to mauve.

Design number: *4212*
Mark: *stamped TEROMA seal*
Artist signature: *F. Gubisch*
Height: *4½ in. (11.5 cm.)*

Vase of squat, waisted form in 'chipped' glass, the interior frosted, painted on the exterior with a sparsely wooded landscape in blotchy shades of green, brown, pink, mauve, and yellow against a yellow shaded ground painted on the interior.

Design number: *3106*
Mark: *painted HANDEL*
Artist signature: *illegible*
Height: *6¾ in. (17 cm.)*

Vase of footed baluster form in 'chipped' glass, the interior polished, painted on the exterior with a lakeland landscape viewed through pine branches in tones of brown, blue, mauve, and yellow, the mottled ground shading to clear at the base.

Design number:     *4205*
Mark:     *stamped TEROMA seal*
Artist signature:     *Loehner*
Height:     *5½ in. (14 cm.)*

Humidor in 'chipped', 'sand-finished' glass, the interior polished, painted on the exterior with a pattern of descending pine branches in 'organic' matte green and gray enamels on a frosted ground, the lid with allover 'organic' matte green enamel.

Design number:     *illegible*
Mark:     *painted HANDEL*
Artist signature:     *Bailey*
Height:     *7½ in. (19 cm.)*

Humidor in 'chipped' glass, the interior polished, painted on the exterior with four colorful birds in flight against a background of leafing bamboo in 'organic' matte green enamel on a frosted ground, the lid with allover 'organic' matte green enamel.

Design number:   *4256*
Mark:            *etched HANDEL in relief*
Artist signature: *etched PALME in relief*
Height:          *9 in. (23 cm.)*

Vase of slender, waisted form in frosted iridescent glass, the interior lightly frosted, the polished exterior etched with a pattern of birds in flight beneath trees in low relief, flashed in pale amber.

Design number:   *4245*
Mark:            *etched HANDEL in relief*
Height:          *6 in. (15 cm.)*

Vase of squat, waisted form in 'chipped' glass, the polished interior partially 'chipped', etched in low relief with a pattern of fruiting vines descending from the rim, flashed in pale amber.

Design number:     *4237*
Mark:              *none*
Artist signature:  *etched MOSHER in relief*
Height:            *11 in. (28 cm.)*

Oviform vase with flared neck in frosted iridescent glass, the interior polished, etched in a design of ferns and wildflowers in low relief, flashed in lustrous amber, with amber rim.

Design number: *4208*
Mark: *stamped TEROMA seal*
Artist signature: *Bedigie*
Height: *8 in. (20 cm.)*

Vase of baluster form in 'chipped', 'sand-finished' glass, the interior polished, painted on the exterior with a dense clump of birch trees in a lakeland landscape in tones of green, yellow, brown, and mauve against a frosted ground.

Design number: *4211*
Mark: *stamped TEROMA seal*
Artist signature: *Bailey*
Height: *6 in. (15 cm.)*

Vase of squat, waisted form, in 'chipped' glass, the interior frosted, painted on the exterior with a sparsely wooded landscape in brown, purple, blue, green, pink, and yellow enamels reflected in a body of water, all against a clear, frosted ground.

Design number:     *4222*
Mark:     *stamped TEROMA seal*
Artist signature:     *Lockrow*
Height:     *8 in. (20 cm.)*

Heavily-walled vase of slender, waisted form in 'chipped' glass, the interior polished, painted on the exterior with a low horizon landscape with birch trees ascending the body in tones of green, brown, and purple against a yellow mottled sky streaked with purple clouds and featuring a bright orange morning sun.

Design number:     *4217*
Mark:     *stamped TEROMA seal*
Artist signature:     *Bedigie*
Height:     *10 in. (25.5 cm.)*

Oviform vase with flaring neck in 'chipped', 'sand-finished' glass, the interior polished, painted on the exterior with birds in flight between birch trees in shades of green, brown, yellow, and blue against a frosted ground.

Design number:     *4219*
Mark:              *stamped HANDEL seal*
Artist signature:  *Broggi*
Height:            *10¾ in. (27.5 cm.)*

Vase of waisted form in 'chipped', 'sand-finished' glass, the interior polished, painted on
the exterior with birch trees in a wooded landscape in shades of green, orange, yellow,
mauve  and blue against a frosted ground.

Design number:    *4213*
Mark:    *painted HANDEL*
Artist signature:    *John Bailey*
Height:    *8½ in. (21.5 cm.)*

Pair of candlesticks in 'chipped' glass, the interior frosted, the spreading bases painted on
the exterior with a windmill in rocky landscape in shades of brown, green, and blue under
a yellow sky shading to mauve, the nozzles with everted 'drip-guards' in pale violet blue.

Design number:     *4204*
Mark:              *stamped TEROMA seal*
Artist signature:  *John Bailey*
Height:            *9 in. (23 cm.)*

Humidor in 'chipped', yellow 'sand-finished' glass, the interior polished, painted on the exterior with a scene of a sailing vessel entering a tropical bay dotted with palm trees and fronds, in shades of russet, green, mauve, and blue against a pale lavender shaded frosted ground, the lid in 'chipped', frosted glass.

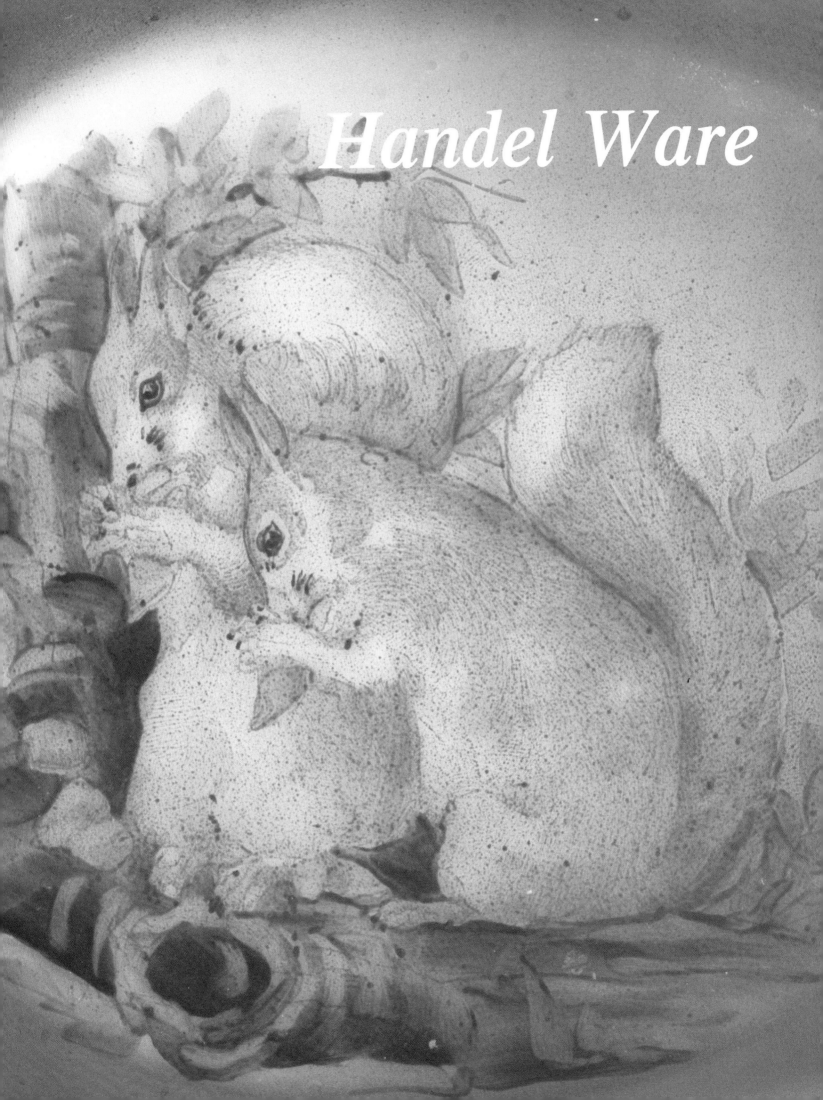

Handel Ware

Design number:    *4091/XF*
Mark:    *stamped HANDEL WARE shield*
Height:    *7½ in. (19 cm.)*

Oviform humidor in opal glass with 'chipped' finish, the base and knopped, hinged cover finished in allover matte 'organic' green enamel, with plain bronzed metal mount and frontal thumbpiece.

*This example retains the original moisture absorbing sponge, held inside the hollow knop of the cover.*

Design number:    *127*
Mark:    *stamped HANDEL WARE shield*
Height:    *4¼ in. (11 cm.)*

Humidor of compressed melon form in opal glass, painted on the exterior in brown and gold, applied with metal collar, the plain gilt metal cover surmounted by a knop in the form of a tobacco pipe resting on its side.

Design number:    *4128/I*
Mark:    *stamped HANDEL WARE shield*
Height:    *6 in. (15 cm.)*

Humidor of downward flaring form in opal glass, painted on the exterior in the Arts & Crafts manner with a village in sparsely wooded landscape in mahogany brown, silhouetted against an olive green mottled sky and pale moon, the flat, hinged cover with plain copper plated metal mount and frontal thumbpiece.

Design number:    *123/274*
Mark:    *stamped HANDEL WARE shield*
Height:    *7½ in. (19 cm.)*

Humidor of dice form in opal glass, realistically painted on the exterior with a scene of two gray squirrels eating nuts while perched on a leafy branch, on a shaded green and russet ground, applied with metal collar, the plain metal cover surmounted by a knop in the form of a reclining young girl wearing a bonnet.

Design number: *4060/F*
Mark: *stamped HANDEL WARE shield*
Height: *7¼ in. (18.5 cm.)*

Squat humidor in opal glass, molded with borders of leaf scrolls in relief, the exterior realistically painted with a portrait of a bearded fisherman in sou'-wester, on a shaded gold and russet ground, the knopped, hinged cover with plain bronzed metal mount and frontal thumb-piece.

Design number: *123/188*
Mark: *stamped HANDEL WARE shield*
Height: *7 in. (18 cm.)*

Humidor of dice form in opal glass, painted on the exterior with a portrait of a monk in pink and sepia tones on a mottled green and russet ground, applied with metal collar, the plain gilt metal cover surmounted by a knop in the form of a tobacco pipe.

Design number: *115/280*
Mark: *stamped HANDEL WARE shield*
Height: *4½ in. (11.5 cm.)*

Mug with loop handle in porcelain, the exterior bat printed with a jolly monk reading a newspaper, in realistic coloration on a brown shaded ground.

Design number: *132/329*
Mark: *stamped HANDEL WARE shield*
Height: *5 in. (13 cm.)*

Squat humidor in opal glass, painted on the exterior with a pair of ducks at pondside in tones of brown and blue on a lime green shaded ground, applied with metal collar, the bronzed metal cover surmounted by a barrel form match strike.

*This example retains the original moisture absorbing sponge, held inside the cover by means of a metal strap.*

Design number: *4091/J*
Mark: *stamped HANDEL WARE shield*
Artist signature: *Kelsey*
Height: *7 in. (18 cm.)*

Oviform humidor in opal glass, painted on the exterior with a stag in mountain landscape in shades of brown, green, and gray on a russet shaded ground, applied with metal collar, the plain bronzed metal cover surmounted by a knop in the form of a tobacco pipe.

Design number:     *4029*
Mark:              *stamped HANDEL WARE shield*
Height:            *4¼ in. (11 cm.)*

Mug with loop handle in porcelain, painted on the exterior with an owl perched on a pine branch with a yellow moon in the background, above the motto 'Many a Time', on a brown ground, the *verso* inscribed with a Shakespearean verse.

Design number:     *4029*
Mark:              *stamped HANDEL WARE shield*
Height:            *4½ in. (11.5 cm.)*

Mug with loop handle in earthenware, painted on the exterior with an owl perched on a pine branch with a yellow moon in the background, above the motto 'Many a Time', on a mahogany brown ground.

Design number:     *4038*
Mark:              *stamped HANDEL WARE shield*
Height:            *3¼ in. (8 cm.)*

Squat humidor in opal glass, painted on the exterior with an owl seated on a pine branch in tones of green and brown on a russet shaded ground, applied with metal collar, the bronzed metal cover surmounted by a barrel form match strike.

Design number:    *111/194*
Mark:    *stamped HANDEL WARE shield*
Height:    *4½ in. (11.5 cm.)*

Mug with loop handle in earthenware, painted on the exterior with an Arab seated on a camel, in green and sepia tones on a shaded green and sandy russet ground, the reverse painted with a crest featuring an Arabic figure mounted with a ruby glass 'jewel' and surmounted by a scimitar.

Design number:    *2379/194*
Mark:    *stamped HANDEL WARE shield*
Height:    *6 in. (15 cm.)*

Cylindrical cigar humidor in opal glass, the base and cover molded with borders of leaf scrolls in relief, painted on the exterior with a crest featuring an Arabic figure mounted with a ruby glass 'jewel' and surmounted by a scimitar, in gilt, green, and russet on a shaded green and russet ground, the reverse painted with an Arab seated on a camel, the flat, hinged cover inscribed *CIGARS* in brown and white enamels beneath a fez, with Greek key patterned bronzed metal mount and ornate frontal thumbpiece.

Design number:    *72/327*
Mark:    *stamped HANDEL WARE shield*
Height:    *6 in. (15 cm.)*

Squat humidor in opal glass, realistically painted on the exterior with an Arab in white robes holding a rifle, and a recumbent camel displaying an intricately patterned saddle on a shaded green and russet ground, the knopped, hinged cover with plain bronzed metal mount and frontal thumbpiece.

Design number:    *4060/M*
Mark:    *stamped HANDEL WARE shield*
Height:    *7¼ in. (18.5 cm.)*

Humidor of downward flaring form in opal glass, realistically painted on the exterior with the head of a stallion with flowing mane on a shaded green and russet ground, the knopped, hinged cover with plain bronzed metal mount and frontal thumbpiece.

Design number:    *4060/G*
Mark:    *stamped HANDEL WARE shield*
Artist signature:    *Rebscher*
Height:    *8 in. (20 cm.)*

Humidor of hexagonal, swelling form in opal glass, molded with borders of leaf scrolls in relief, realistically painted on the exterior with a brown bear on a leafing tree branch against a shaded green and russet ground, the knopped, hinged cover with plain bronzed metal mount and frontal thumbpiece.

Design number: *460/324*
Mark: *stamped HANDEL WARE shield*
Height: *4½ in. (11.5 cm.)*

Cylindrical cigarette jar in opal glass, the rim molded with leaf scrolls in relief, realistically painted on the exterior with a bridled horse's head, in tones of brown on a shaded green and russet ground, the gilt metal cover with beaded rim and beaded, loop knop.

Design number: *4091/1*
Mark: *stamped HANDEL WARE shield*
Artist signature: *Kelsey*
Height: *7 in. (18 cm.)*

Humidor of dice form in opal glass, realistically painted on the exterior with the heads of a bridled horse and a hunting dog on a shaded green and russet ground, applied with metal collar, the plain gilt metal cover surmounted by a knop in the form of a tobacco pipe.

Design number:    *104/331*
Mark:    *stamped HANDEL WARE shield*
Height:    *6 in. (15 cm.)*

Cylindrical cigar humidor in opal glass molded with borders of leaf scrolls in relief, realistically painted on the exterior with two brown bear cubs clambering on a tree stump with green leafage in the background, on a shaded russet and gold ground, the flat, hinged cover with Greek key patterned gilt metal mount and ornate frontal thumbpiece.

Design number:    *4091/F*
Mark:    *stamped HANDEL WARE shield*
Artist signature:    *Godwin*
Height:    *6 in. (15 cm.)*

Squat humidor in opal glass, realistically painted on the exterior with a portrait of a stag and doe on a green and russet shaded ground, the knopped, hinged cover with plain bronzed metal mount and frontal thumbpiece.

Design number:    *4091/H*
Mark:    *stamped HANDEL WARE shield*
Height:    *6 in. (15 cm.)*

Cylindrical cigar humidor in opal glass molded with borders of leaf scrolls in relief, realistically painted on the exterior with the bridled head of a horse on a shaded russet ground, the flat, hinged cover with Greek key patterned bronzed metal mount and ornate frontal thumbpiece.

Smokers' companion set, in metal mounted opal glass, with realistically painted decoration of a hound with bagged game on a green, russet, and tan shaded ground, comprising:

Design number:   *4128*
Mark:            *stamped HANDEL WARE shield*
Height:          *6 in. (15 cm.)*


Cylindrical cigar humidor molded with borders of leaf scrolls in relief, the flat, hinged cover with Greek key patterned bronzed metal mount and ornate frontal thumbpiece.

Design number:   *none*
Mark:            *stamped HANDEL WARE shield*
Height:          *2¼ in. (5.5 cm.)*


Bulbous matchsafe with bronzed metal collar ridged to function as a striker.

Design number:   *none*
Mark:            *printed retailers mark on base:*
                 *Compliments of*
                 *Louis Stream, Tobacconist,*
                 *48 E. 42 St., NYC*
Diameter:        *4½ in. (11.5 cm.)*

Ashtray of compressed form, mounted with bronzed metal collar applied with foliate cigarette rests.

Design number:     *4129/Q*
Mark:              *stamped HANDEL WARE shield*
Height:            *6½ in. (16.5 cm.)*


Humidor of inverted thistle form in opal glass, realistically painted on the exterior with a scene of two hunting hounds in a forest in tones of brown, green and gray, the knopped, hinged cover with plain bronzed metal mount and frontal thumbpiece.


Design number:     *89/128*
Mark:              *stamped HANDEL WARE shield*
Height:            *7½ in. (19 cm.)*


Oviform humidor in opal glass, realistically painted on the exterior with a pair of hunting hounds standing in a meadow in tones of brown, green and russet, the knopped, hinged cover inscribed *TOBACCO* in brown and white enamels, and with florette-patterned bronzed metal mount and ornate frontal thumbpiece.


Design number:     *4091/G*
Mark:              *stamped HANDEL WARE shield*
Artist signature:  *Bauer*
Height:            *6½ in. (16.5 cm.)*


Humidor of inverted thistle form in opal glass, realistically painted on the exterior with five leaping hunting hounds on a green and russet shaded ground, the knopped, hinged cover with plain gilt metal mount and frontal thumbpiece.

A selection of opal glass objects, realistically painted on the exterior with pug dogs wearing red collars, including:

Design number:    *4091/S*
Mark:              *stamped HANDEL WARE shield*
Artist signature:  *Kelsey*
Diameter:          *4¾ in. (12 cm.)*

Design number:    *4091/S*
Mark:              *stamped HANDEL WARE shield*
Artist signature:  *Bauer*
Diameter:          *4¾ in. (12 cm.)*

Two ashtrays of compressed form, mounted with bronzed metal collars applied with foliate cigarette rests.

Design number:    *none*
Mark:              *none*
Height:            *2¼ in. (5.5 cm.)*

Creamer with loop handle shaded russet at the rim, the *verso* stamped: *CAFE MELLONE—NEW HAVEN, CONN.—RESTAURANT DELUXE—TABLE D'HOTE & A LA CARTE.*

Design number:    *4091/F*
Mark:              *stamped HANDEL WARE shield*
Artist signature:  *Bauer*
Height:            *5¾ in. (14.5 cm.)*

Squat humidor with green and russet shaded ground, the knopped, hinged cover with plain bronzed metal mount and frontal thumbpiece.

Detail of cover on design number    *2379/140*

Design number:    *2379/140*
Mark:    *stamped HANDEL WARE shield with ribbon*
Height:    *6 in. (15 cm.)*

Cylindrical cigar humidor in opal glass, the base and cover molded with borders of leaf scrolls in relief, realistically painted on the exterior with a gentleman golfer and caddy on the fairway on a shaded green and russet ground, the flat, hinged cover inscribed *CIGARS* in brown and white enamels beneath a scene of golfers on the putting green, with scroll-patterned metal mount.

Design number: *475/160*
Mark: *stamped HANDEL WARE shield with ribbon*
Diameter: *6 in. (15 cm.)*

Ashtray of compressed round form in opal glass, painted on the exterior with a scene of a gentleman golfer and his caddy, in shades of blue, brown, red, white and green on a green and tan mottled ground, the applied bronzed metal rim with anthemion scroll handles and beaded cigarette rest.

Design number: *none*
Mark: *none*
Height: *3 in. (7.5 cm.)*

Bulbous ash receiver in opal glass, painted on the exterior with a scene of a lady and gentleman playing golf while a caddy looks on, in shades of tan, blue, white, gray and green on a green and tan shaded ground, with gilt metal rim and banded metal base on four scroll feet.

Design number:     155/325
Mark:              stamped HANDEL WARE shield
Height:            6½ in. (16.5 cm.)


Humidor of inverted thistle form in opal glass, realistically painted on the exterior with a portrait of an Indian chief in full headdress on a shaded green and russet ground, the knopped, hinged cover with plain bronzed metal mount and frontal thumbpiece.


Design number:     4091/H
Mark:              stamped HANDEL WARE shield
Height:            6 in. (15 cm.)


Cylindrical cigar humidor in opal glass, molded with borders of leaf scrolls in relief, realistically painted on the exterior with a portrait of an Indian chief in full headdress on a shaded green and russet ground, the flat, hinged cover with Greek key patterned bronzed metal mount and ornate frontal thumbpiece.

Design number: *89/130*
Mark: *stamped HANDEL WARE shield*
Height: *7½ in. (19 cm.)*

Oviform humidor in opal glass, realistically painted on the exterior with a half-length portrait of an Indian brave clad in buckskin, on a shaded green, russet and tan ground, the knopped, hinged cover inscribed *TOBACCO* in brown and white enamels, with florette-patterned metal mount and ornate frontal thumbpiece.

Design number: *72/282*
Mark: *stamped HANDEL WARE shield*
Height: *5¾ in. (14.5 cm.)*

Squat humidor in opal glass, realistically painted on the exterior with a portrait of an Indian chief in wide-brimmed hat on a shaded green and russet ground, the knopped, hinged cover inscribed *TOBACCO* in brown and white enamels, with florette-patterned metal mount and ornate frontal thumbpiece.

*This example retains the original retailer's price label for $2.50.*

Design number: *87/131*
Mark: *painted script signature*
Height: *8 in. (20 cm.)*


Humidor of hexagonal, swelling form in opal glass, realistically painted on the exterior with a portrait of a squatting Indian and squaw, on a shaded green and russet ground, the knopped, hinged cover inscribed *TOBACCO* in brown and white enamels, with florette-patterned bronzed metal mount and ornate frontal thumbpiece.


Design number: *2379/131*
Mark: *stamped HANDEL decorator mark*
Height: *6 in. (15 cm.)*


Cylindrical cigar humidor in opal glass, the base and cover molded with borders of leaf scrolls in relief, realistically painted on the exterior with a portrait of a squatting Indian and squaw, on a shaded green and russet ground, the flat, hinged cover inscribed *CIGARS* in russet and white enamels, beneath a still life of Indian artifacts, with scroll-patterned, bronzed metal mount and ornate frontal thumbpiece.


Design number: *86/131*
Mark: *stamped HANDEL decorator mark*
Height: *7¼ in. (18.5 cm.)*


Humidor of downward flaring form in opal glass, realistically painted on the exterior with a portrait of a squatting Indian and squaw on a shaded green and russet ground, the knopped, hinged cover inscribed *TOBACCO* in brown and white enamels, with florette-patterned bronzed metal mount and ornate frontal thumbpiece.

Smokers' companion set, in metal mounted opal glass, each piece with realistically painted Indian portrait in full headdress on a green and russet shaded ground, comprising:

Design number:  *480/202*
Mark:           *stamped HANDEL WARE shield*
Dimensions:     *5½ in. × 4½ in. (14 cm. × 11.5 cm.)*

Ashtray of compressed, rectangular form with gilt metal rim applied with foliate cigarette rests.

Design number:  *none*
Mark:           *none*
Height:         *2¼ in. (5.5 cm.)*

Bulbous matchsafe with bronzed metal collar ridged to function as a striker, inscribed *MATCHES* on the *verso*.

Design number:  *89/130*
Mark:           *stamped HANDEL WARE shield*
Height:         *7½ in. (19 cm.)*

Oviform humidor with knopped, hinged cover inscribed *TOBACCO* in russet and white enamels, with florette-patterned metal mount and ornate frontal thumbpiece.

" . . . Beauty never leaves a Handel Lamp. She
hovers over it while it stands silent under the
casement moon. She revels in its soft,
glowing colors as the light streams through
the hand-wrought shade. In vain she
challenges daylight to take away its
charm . . ."

From a Handel Company
advertisement of 1916